THE HUNCHBACK OF NOTRE DAME

The Hunchback of Notre Dame

VICTOR HUGO

NEW ENGLISH LIBRARY
TIMES MIRROR

Abridged

*

FIRST NEL PAPERBACK EDITION DECEMBER 1976

*

NEL Books are published by
New English Library Limited from Barnard's Inn, Holborn, London EC1N 2JR
Made and printed in Great Britain by Hunt Barnard Printing Ltd., Aylesbury, Bucks.

45003234 5

BOOK ONE

1

One morning, three hundred and forty-eight years, six months and nineteen days ago, the Parisians were awakened by a grand peal from all the bells, within the triple enclosure of the City, the University and the Town.

Yet the 6th of January, 1482, was not a day of which history has preserved any record. There was nothing remarkable in the event that so early in the morning set in commotion the bells and the bourgeois of Paris.

But on this 6th of January, what 'set in motion the whole *populaire* of Paris', was the fact of its being a double holiday, the Epiphany, or Feast of the Kings, and the *Fête des fous*, or Feast of the Fools. To celebrate such a day there was to be a bonfire kindled on the Place de Grève, a maypole raised at the Chapelle de Braque, and a mystery performed in the Palace of Justice. Proclamation had been made the evening before, in all the public squares.

Crowds of people had accordingly been flocking all the morning, their houses and shops shut up, from all quarters of the town towards one of the three places appointed. Everyone had made his selection – the bonfire, the maypole, or the mystery. The greatest crowds, however, were to be found on the approaches to the Palace of Justice, because it was known that the Flemish ambassadors, who had arrived two days previously, intended to be present, not only at the performance of the mystery, but also at the election of the Fools' Pope, which was likewise to take place in the Great Hall.

On that day it was no easy matter to make one's way into the Great Hall. The open square in front of the Palace, thronged with people, presented to the gazers from the windows the aspect of a sea into which five or six streets, like the mouths of so many rivers, every moment discharged fresh floods of human heads. The waves of this deluge, constantly increasing, broke against the angles of the houses that projected here and there, like so many promontories, into the irregularly shaped basin of the square.

At the doors, at the windows, at the skylights, and on the roofs, swarmed thousands of good-natured *bourgeois* faces, looking calmly and quietly at the Palace, at the crowd, and asking nothing more to look at; for many honest Paris folks are quite content with gazing at the gazers, and can even regard a wall with intense interest when they think there is something going on behind it.

The play was not to begin until the great clock of the Palace had struck the last stroke announcing noon. This was, no doubt, rather late for a mystery, but as ambassadors were to be present their convenience was to be regarded.

The most of the crowd had been waiting all the morning. A good many of these honest sight-seers had shivered on the grand staircase at daybreak; some even insisted that they had passed the night close to the great doorway so as to make sure of being the first to enter. The crowd, continually increasing, became by degrees too great for the room and, like a river overflowing its banks, began to rise along the walls, to swell around the pillars, and even inundate the window-sills, the tops of the columns, the cornices and every projection of the sculptures. The noise made by a crowd so squeezed, packed, crushed, trodden on, smothered, began to assume a tone of decided acrimony.

There was, amongst others, a group of joyous rascals who, after breaking the glass of a window, had established themselves boldly upon the entablature, and from there cast their looks and their railleries alternately within and without, upon the crowd in the Hall and the crowd out of doors. From their mimicry of well-known personages, their flippant remarks exchanged with their comrades from one end of the Hall to the other, and their uproarious laughter, it was easy to see that these young students, far from participating in the general languor or vexation, were enjoying themselves heartily by making so much out of one spectacle that they never minded waiting for another.

'Upon my soul, it's you, Joannes Frollo de Molendino!' cried a friend in the crowd to a little blond with a pretty and malicious face straddled on the capital of one of the lofty columns. 'Hello! Jack of the windmill! You are well named today, anyway, for your two legs and your two arms keep moving like the four sails that go in the wind. How long have you been perched up there?'

'Four hours at least, by the devil's mercy,' answered Joannes. 'I hope they will be put to my credit in purgatory. I heard the beginning of the high mass sung in the Sainte Chapelle by the King of Sicily's eight chanters.'

At that moment it struck twelve.

'Ha!' exclaimed the whole crowd, with one voice of satisfaction.

The scholars became quiet.

They waited one – two – three – five minutes a quarter of an hour – but nothing came. Meanwhile impatience was succeeded by displeasure. Angry words began to circulate, though as yet only in whispers. 'The mystery! the mystery!' was uttered. A storm, which as yet only growled, was agitating the surface of that human sea. It was our friend Jehan du Moulin that elicited the first explosion.

'The mystery! and the devil take the Flemings!' cried he, with the whole force of his lungs, twisting himself, like a serpent, about his pillar.

The multitude clapped their hands. 'The mystery!' they all shouted, 'and let Flanders go to all the devils!'

'We must have the mystery immediately!' resumed the scholar; 'or my advice is that we hang the bailiff of the Palace in the way of comedy and morality.'

A great acclamation followed. The four poor devils of sergeants began to turn pale and look anxiously at each other. The multitude pressed toward them, and they already saw the slight wooden balustrade which separated them from the crowd bending inward under the pressure.

The moment was critical.

At that instant the hangings of the dressing-room were lifted, giving passage to a personage, the mere sight of whom sufficed to stop the eager multitude, and change their anger into curiosity as if by enchantment.

'Silence! silence!' was the cry from all sides.

The personage, but little reassured, and trembling in every limb, advanced to the edge of the marble table, making a profusion of bows, which, the nearer he approached approximated more and more to genuflexions.

Calm, however, was gradually restored. Only that slight murmur was heard which is always exhaled from the silence of a great crowd.

'Messieurs les bourgeois,' said he, 'and mesdemoiselles les bourgeoises, we shall have the honor of declaiming and performing before his eminence monsieur le cardinal, a very fine morality, entitled *The Good Judgment of Madame the Virgin Mary*. I play Jupiter. His eminence is at this moment accompanying the most honorable embassy from monsieur the Duke of Austria, which is at this moment detained by hearing the harangue of monsieur the rector of the University, at the Baudets gate. As soon as the most eminent cardinal is arrived, we shall begin.'

It is certain that nothing less than the intervention of Jupiter was necessary to save the four unhappy sergeants of the bailiff of the Palace.

While, however, Jupiter was delivering his harangue, the satisfaction, the admiration unanimously excited by his costume, were dissipated by his words; and when he arrived at that unhappy conclusion, 'as soon as the most eminent cardinal is arrived, we shall begin,' his voice was lost in a thunder of hooting.

'Begin immediately! The mystery! the mystery at once!' cried the people.

Poor Jupiter, haggard, frightened, pale under his rouge, let fall his thunderbolts, took his bicoquet in his hand; then, bowing and trembling, he stammered: 'His eminence – the ambassadors – Madame Margaret of Flanders' – he knew not what to say.

The fact was, he was afraid he should be hanged – hanged by the populace for waiting, or hanged by the cardinal for not having waited – on either hand he beheld an abyss, that is to say, a gallows.

Happily, someone came forward to extricate him and assume the responsibility.

An individual who stood within the railing, in the space which it left clear around the marble table, and whom no one had yet perceived, so completely was his long and slender person sheltered from every visual ray by the diameter of the pillar against which he had set his back – this individual, we say, tall, thin, pale, light complexioned – still young, though wrinkles were already visible in his forehead and his cheeks – with sparkling eyes and a smiling mouth – clad in a garment of black serge, threadbare and shining with age – approached the marble table, and made a sign to the poor sufferer. But the other, in his perturbation, did not observe it.

The newcomer advanced another step forward.

'Jupiter,' said he, 'my dear Jupiter!'

'Who calls me?' said Jupiter.

'I do,' answered the personage clad in black – it was the author.

'Ah!' exclaimed Jupiter.

'Begin directly,' returned the other; 'satisfy the people, and I take upon myself to appease monsieur the bailiff, who will appease monsieur the cardinal.'

Jupiter now took breath. 'Messeigneurs les bourgeois,' cried he, at the utmost stretch of his lungs, to the multitude who continued to hoot him, 'we are going to begin directly.'

Then followed a deafening clapping of hands, and the hall shook with acclamation.

A music of high and low-keyed instruments now struck up underneath the stage; the hangings were lifted, and four characters in motley attire, with painted faces, issued forth, clambered up the steep ladder already mentioned, and reaching the upper platform, drew up in line before the audience, whom they saluted with a profound obeisance, whereupon the musical sounds ceased and the mystery began.

The four characters commenced, amidst a profound silence, the delivery of a prologue, which we gladly spare the reader. However, as is still the case in our own time, the audience paid more attention to the gowns they wore than to the parts they were enacting – and in truth they did right.

Meanwhile, in all that assemblage upon which the four allegorical personages seemed to be striving which could pour out the most copious floods of metaphor, no ear was so attentive, no heart so palpitating, no eye so eager, no neck so outstretched, as were the eye, ear, neck and heart of the author, the poet, the brave Pierre Gringoire.

He had retired a few paces behind his pillar again; and there it was that he listened, looked and enjoyed. The benevolent plaudits which had greeted the opening of his prologue still resounded in his breast; and he was completely absorbed in that species of ecstatic contemplation with which a dramatic author marks his ideas falling one by one from the lips of the actor, amid the silence of a crowded audience.

3

Poor Gringoire! The noise of all the great double petards let off on Saint John's day – the discharge of a score of crooked arquebusses – would have split his ears less violently at that solemn and dramatic moment, than the few words that now came from the lips of an usher, 'His Eminence Monsieur, the Cardinal of Bourbon.'

His fears were these. The entrance of his Eminence disorganized the audience completely. All eyes were turned toward the gallery, and there was a general buzz: 'The cardinal! the cardinal!' repeated every tongue.

The cardinal stopped a moment upon the threshold of the gallery; and while casting his eyes with great indifference over the assemblage the tumult redoubled. Each one wished to obtain a better view of him. Each one stretching his neck over his neighbor's shoulder.

He entered, saluted the company with that hereditary smile which the great have always in readiness for the people, and moved slowly towards his armchair of crimson velvet placed for his reception, looking as if some other matter occupied his mind.

As for the students, they swore. It was their own day – their Feast of Fools – their saturnalia – the annual orgies of the basoche (Lawyers' clerks of the Paliament of Paris) and the schools. All was permissible that day. And then there were numberless wanton hussies among the crowd – Simone Quatre-livres, Agnès-la-Gadine, Robine Pièdebou. Was it not the least that could be expected, that they should swear at their ease, and profane God's name a little, on such a day as that, in such a goodly company of churchmen and courtezans? And accordingly, they did not mince matters; but amidst the uproarious applause a frightful din of blasphemies and obscenities proceeded from all those tongues let loose, those tongues of clerks and scholars, tied up all the rest of the year by the fear of Saint Louis's branding-iron.

4

From the moment at which the cardinal entered, Gringoire had been incessantly exerting himself for the salvation of his prologue. He had first enjoined the actors, who were waiting in suspense, to proceed, and raise their voices; then, finding that no one listened, he had stopped them; and for nearly a quarter of an hour, during which the interruption had continued, he had been constantly beating with his foot and gesticulating, and urging those near him to have the prologue proceeded with – but all in vain. No one could be turned aside from the cardinal, the embassy and the gallery – the sole centre of that vast circle of visual rays.

Nevertheless, when our poet saw tranquility a little restored, he bethought himself of a stratagem which might have saved the performance.

'Monsieur,' said he, turning to one of his neighbors, of fair round figure, with a patient-looking countenance, 'suppose they were to begin again?'

'Begin what?' said the man.

'Why, the mystery,' said Gringoire.

'Just as you please,' returned the other.

This demi-approbation was enough for Gringoire, and taking the affair into his own hands, he began to call out, confounding himself at the same time as much as possible with the crowd. 'Begin the mystery again! – begin again!'

But it was of no use. It seemed as if, at the cardinal's entrance, some invisible and magical thread had suddenly drawn away every look from the marble table to the gallery, from the southern extremity of the hall to its western side. Nothing could disenchant the audience; all eyes remained fixed in that direction; and the persons who successively arrived, and their cursed names, and their faces, and their dresses, made a continual diversion. The case was desperate.

With what bitterness did he see all his fabric of poetry and of glory thus falling to pieces! Only to think that this multitude had been on the point of rebelling against monsieur the bailiff through their impatience to hear his composition: and now that they had it, they were indifferent about it.

The usher's brutal monologue ceased at last; everybody had arrived: so that Gringoire took breath; and the actors were going on bravely, when Maître Coppenole, a hosier, rose suddenly, and Gringoire heard him deliver, in the midst of the universal attention to his piece, this abominable harangue:

'Messieurs the citizens and squires of Paris – by the Holy Rood! I know not what we be doing here. I do indeed see, down in that corner, upon that stage, some people who look as if they wanted to fight. I know not whether that be what you call a mystery; but I do know that 'tis not amusing. For this quarter of an hour I've been waiting the first blow – but nothing comes – they're cowards, and maul one another but with foul words. You should have had boxers from London or Rotterdam. Aye! then indeed we should have had hard knocks, which you might have heard even out upon the square – but those creatures there are pitiful. They should at least give us a Morris-dance or some other piece of mummery. This is not what I was told it was to be – I'd been promised a feast of fools with an election of the Lord of Misrule. We at Ghent, too, have our Fools' Pope; and in that, by the Rood! we're behind nobody. But we do thus: – a mob comes together, as here for instance; then each in his turn goes and puts his head through a hole and makes faces at the others; he who makes the ugliest face according to general acclamation, is chosen pope. That's our way, and it's very diverting.

11

Shall we make your pope after the fashion of my country? At any rate it will be less tiresome than listening to those babblers. If they've a mind to come and try their hands at face-making, they shall be in the game. What say ye, my masters? Here's a droll sample enough of both sexes to give us a right hearty Flemish laugh, and we can show ugly mugs enough to give us hopes of a fine grinning-match.'

Gringoire would fain have replied, but amazement, resentment, and indignation deprived him of speech. Besides, the motion made by the popular hosier was received with such enthusiasm by those townsfolk, flattered at being called squires, that all resistance would have been useless. All he could now do was to go with the stream. Gringoire hid his face with both his hands.

5

In the twinkling of an eye, everything was ready for putting Coppenole's idea into execution. Townspeople, students and clerks had all set themselves to work. The small chapel, situated opposite to the marble table, was fixed upon to be the scene of the grimaces. The glass being broken out of one of the divisions of the pretty rose-shaped window over the doorway, left free a circle of stone through which it was agreed that the candidates should put their heads. To reach it they had to climb upon two casks which had been laid hold of somewhere and placed one upon another. It was settled that each candidate, whether man or woman (for they might make a popess), in order to leave fresh and entire the impression of their grimace, should cover their faces and keep themselves unseen in the chapel until the moment of making their appearance. In less than an instant the chapel was filled with competitors, and the door was closed upon them.

The grimaces commenced. The first face that appeared at the hole, with eyelids turned up to show the red, cavernous mouth, and a forehead wrinkled in like our hussar boots in the time of the Empire, excited an inextinguishable burst of laughter. A second face, and a third, succeeded – then another – then another – the spectators each time laughing and stamping their feet with delight.

There was no longer any distinction of scholars, ambassadors, townspeople, men, or women. The Grande Salle had become, as it were, one vast furnace of audacity and joviality, in which every mouth was a shout, every face a grimace, every figure a posture –

the sum total howling and roaring. The strange visages that came one after another to grind their teeth at the broken window were like so many fresh brands cast upon the fire; and from all that effervescent multitude there escaped, as the exhalation of the furnace, a noise, sharp, penetrating, like the buzzing of the wings of gnats.

As for Gringoire – as soon as the first moment of depression was over, he had regained his self-possession. He had hardened himself against adversity. 'Go on,' he said for the third time to his players – who, after all, were mere talking machines – then he strode up and down before the marble table; he felt tempted to go and take his turn at the hole in the chapel-window, if only to have the pleasure of making faces at the ungrateful people. 'But no – that would be unworthy of us – no revenge – let us struggle to the last,' muttered he to himself – 'the power of poetry over the people is great – I will bring them back. We will see which of the two shall prevail – grimaces or belles-lettres.'

Alas! he was left the sole spectator of his play.

'Noël! Noël! Noël!' cried the people from all sides.

It was indeed a miraculous grin that now beamed through the Gothic aperture. After all the figures which had succeeded each other at the window, without realizing that idea of the grotesque which had formed itself in the imagination of the people heated by the orgie, it required nothing less to gain their votes than the sublime grimace which now dazzled the assemblage. We shall not attempt to give the reader an idea of that tetrahedron nose – that horse-shoe mouth – that small left eye over-shadowed by a red bushy brow, while the right eye disappeared entirely under a monstrous wart – of those straggling teeth with breaches here and there like the battlements of a fortress – of that horny lip, over which one of those teeth projected like the tusk of an elephant – of that forked chin – and, above all, of the expression diffused over the whole – that mixture of malice, astonishment and melancholy. Imagination alone can picture this combination.

The acclamation was unanimous; the crowd precipitated itself toward the chapel, and the happy Lord of Misrule was led out in triumph. And now the surprise and admiration of the people redoubled. They found the wondrous grin to be but his ordinary face.

Or rather, his whole person was a grimace. His large head, bristling with red hair – between his shoulders an enormous hump, to which he had a corresponding projection in front; a framework of thighs and legs, so strangely gone astray that they touched only at the knees, and when viewed in front, looked like

13

two sickles joined together by the handles – sprawling feet – monstrous hands – and yet, with all that deformity, a certain awe-inspiring vigor, agility and courage – strange exception to the everlasting rule which prescribes that strength, like beauty, shall result from harmony. Such was the pope whom the fools had just chosen.

One would have said a giant that had been broken and awkwardly mended.

When he appeared on the threshold of the chapel, motionless, squat, almost as broad as he was high, the populace recognized him at once by his coat, half red and half violet, figured over with little silver bells, and still more by the perfection of his ugliness – and exclaimed with one voice: 'It's Quasimodo the bell-ringer! It's Quasimodo the hunchback of Notre-Dame! Quasimodo the one-eyed! Quasimodo the bandy-legged! Noël! Noël!'

The poor devil, it seems, had a choice of surnames.

Quasimodo, the object of the tumult, stood in the doorway of the chapel, gloomy and grave, letting himself be admired.

Maître Coppenole, wondering, went up to him. 'By the Rood! Holy Father! why, thou hast the prettiest ugliness I did ever see in my life! Thou wouldst deserve to be pope at Rome as well as at Paris.'

So saying, he clapped his hand merrily upon the other's shoulder. Quasimodo never moved. Coppenole continued: 'Thou art a fellow with whom I long to feast, though it should cost me a new douzain of twelve livres tournois. What say'st thou to it?'

Quasimodo made no answer.

'By the Holy Rood!' cried the hosier, 'art thou deaf?'

He was indeed deaf.

However, he began to be impatient at Coppenole's manners, and he all at once turned toward him with so formidable a grinding of his teeth that the Flemish giant recoiled like a bull-dog before a cat.

A circle of terror and respect was instantly made round this strange personage. And an old woman explained to Maître Coppenole that Quasimodo was deaf.

'Deaf?' cried the hosier, with his boisterous Flemish laugh. 'Holy Rood! then he's a pope indeed!'

'Ho! I know him,' cried Jehan, who was at last come down from his capital to have a nearer look at Quasimodo; 'it's my brother the archdeacon's bell-ringer. Good-day to you, Quasimodo.'

Meanwhile, all the beggars, all the lackeys, all the cutpurses, together with the students, had gone in procession to fetch from the wardrobe of the clerks the pasteboard tiara and the mock robe

14

appropriated to the Fools' Pope or Lord of Misrule. Quasimodo allowed himself to be dressed in them without a frown, and with a sort of proud docility. They then seated him upon a parti-colored litter. Twelve officers of the brotherhood of Fools, laying hold of the poles that were attached to it, hoisted him upon their shoulders; and a sort of bitter and disdainful joy seemed to overspread his sullen face when he beheld under his deformed feet all those heads of handsome and well-shaped men. Then the whole bawling and tattered procession set forth to make, according to custom, the inner circuit of the galleries of the Palace, before parading through the streets and squares.

6

We are delighted to inform our readers that during all this scene Gringoire and his piece had held out. His actors, goaded on by himself, had not ceased spouting their parts, nor had he ceased to listen. He had resigned himself to the uproar, and was deter-mined to go on to the end, not despairing of a return of public attention. This gleam of hope revived when he saw Quasimodo, Coppenole, and the noisy train of the Fools' Pope march with great clamor out of the hall. The rest of the crowd rushing eagerly after them. 'Good!' said he to himself – 'there go all the marplots at last!' But, unfortunately, all the hare-brained people composed the audience. In a twinkling the great hall was almost empty.

'Comrades!' suddenly cried one of the young fellows in the windows, 'Esmeralda! Esmeralda is in the Square!'

This word produced a magical effect. All who remained in the hall rushed toward the windows, climbing up the walls to see, and repeating, 'Esmeralda! Esmeralda!'

At the same time a great noise of applause was heard without.

'What do they mean by Esmeralda?' said Gringoire, clasping his hands in despair. 'Heavens! it seems to be the turn of the windows now!'

He turned toward the marble table, and saw that the per-formance was interrupted.

'The devil take you all!' said he to the players; 'and if they pay me I'll pay you.'

Then he made his retreat, hanging his head, but the last in the field, like a general who has fought well.

BOOK TWO

1

The night comes on early in January. The streets were already growing dark when Gringoire quitted the Palace. This nightfall pleased him; he longed to reach some obscure and solitary alley, that he might there meditate at his ease, and that the philosopher might lay the first healing balm to the wounds of the poet. Philosophy was, indeed, his only refuge, for he knew not where to find a lodging place. After the signal failure of his first dramatic attempt, he dared not return to that which he occupied, having reckoned upon what the provost was to give him for his play to enable him to pay the six months' rent which he owed.

Then he took a desperate resolution. It was to plunge boldly into the very heart of the illumination, and go to the Place de Grève.

'At least,' thought he, 'I shall perhaps get a brand to warm my fingers at the bonfire; and I shall manage to sup on some morsel from the three great shields of royal sugar that were to be set out on the public refectory.'

2

When Pierre Gringoire arrived at the Place de Grève he was benumbed with cold. He had gone over the Miller's Bridge to avoid the crowd on the Pont au Change and Jehan Fourbault's banners; but the wheels of all the bishop's mills had splashed him as he crossed, so that his coat was wet through; and it seemed to him that the fate of his piece had rendered him even colder. Accordingly, he hurried toward the bonfire which burned magnificently in the middle of the Place; a considerable crowd, however, encircled it.

'You villainous Parisians!' said he to himself (for Gringoire, like a true dramatic poet, was addicted to monologues), 'so, now you keep me from the fire! And yet I've good need of a chimney-corner. My shoes are sponges in the water – and then, all those execrable mills have been raining upon me. Let us see, now, if any of those lazy rascals will disturb themselves. What are they doing there the while? Warming themselves – a fine pleasure, truly!'

On looking nearer, however, he perceived that the circle of people was much wider than was requisite to warm themselves at the bonfire, and was not attracted alone by the beauty of a hundred blazing bundles.

In a wide space left clear between the fire and the crowd, a young girl was dancing.

She was not tall, but the elasticity of her slender shape made her appear so. She was a brunette, but it was obvious that in the daylight her complexion would have that golden gleam seen upon the women of Spain and of Rome. Her tiny foot, as well, was Andalusian, for it was at once tight and at ease in its light and graceful sandal. She was dancing, turning, whirling upon an antique Persian carpet spread negligently under her feet; and each time as she turned and her radiant countenance passed before you, her large black eyes seemed to flash upon you.

Every look was fixed upon her, every mouth was open in the circle about her; and, indeed, while she danced to the sound of the tambourine which her two round and delicate arms lifted above her head; slender, fragile, active as a wasp; with her golden girdle without a fold; her skirt of varied colors swelling out below her slender waist, giving momentary glimpses of her fine-formed legs; her round bared shoulders; her black hair and her sparkling eyes; she looked like something more than human.

She took up from the ground two swords, the points of which she supported upon her forehead, making them whirl in one direction, while she turned in the other. She was indeed no other than a gypsy. The bonfire cast upon her a red flaring light, which flickered brightly upon the circle of faces of the crowd and the brown forehead of the young girl, and, at the extremities of the Square threw a wan reflection, mingled with the wavering shadows – on one side, upon the old dark wrinkled front of the Maison aux Piliers – on the other, upon the stone arms of the gibbet.

Among the thousand faces tinged by the scarlet light, there was one which seemed to be more than all the rest absorbed in contemplation of the dancer. It was the face of a man, austere, calm and sombre. This man, whose costume was hidden by the crowd that surrounded him, seemed to be not more than thirty-five years of age; yet he was bald, having only a few thin tufts of hair about his temples, which were already gray; his broad and high forehead was beginning to be furrowed with wrinkles; but in his deep-set eyes there shone an extraordinary youth, an intense animation, a depth of passion. He kept them constantly fixed upon the gypsy; and while the giddy young girl of sixteen danced and swung to the delight of all, his reverie seemed to grow more and more gloomy. From time to time a smile and a sigh met each other on his lips; but the smile was far more sad than the sigh.

The girl, breathless, stopped at last, while the crowd lovingly applauded.

'Djali!' cried the gypsy.

Gringoire then saw come up to her a little white goat, alert, brisk and glossy, with gilt horns, gilt hoofs and a gilt collar, which he had not before observed, because until that moment it had been lying crouched upon one corner of the carpet, looking at her mistress dance.

'Djali,' said the dancer, 'it's your turn now,' and sitting down, she gracefully held out her tambourine to the goat.

'Djali,' she continued, 'what month of the year is this?'

The animal lifted its fore-foot and struck one stroke upon the tambourine. It was, in fact, the first month of the year. The crowd applauded.

'Djali!' resumed the girl, turning her tambourine another way, 'what day of the month is it?'

Djali lifted her little golden foot, and struck six times upon the tambourine.

The people were wonderstruck.

'There is witchcraft in all that,' said a sinister voice in the crowd. It was that of the bald man who had his eyes constantly upon the gypsy.

She shuddered and turned around. But the applause burst forth again and smothered the sinister exclamation.

Indeed, they so completely effaced it from her mind, that she continued to interrogate her goat.

'Djali!' said she, 'how does Maître Guichard Grand-Remy, captain of the town pistoliers, go in the procession at Candlemas?'

Djali reared on her hind legs and began to bleat, marching at the same time with so seemly a gravity that the whole circle of spectators burst into a laugh at this parody of the hypocritical devotion of the captain of pistoliers.

'Sacrilege! profanation!' cried the voice of the bald-headed man.

The gypsy turned round again.

'Ah!' said she, 'it's that ugly man!' Then putting out her lower lip beyond the upper one she made a little pouting grimace which seemed familiar to her, turned upon her heel, and began to collect in her tambourine the contributions of the multitude.

Big pieces of silver, little pieces of silver, pennies and farthings were now showered upon her. In taking her round, she all at once came in front of Gringoire; and as he, in perfect absence of mind, thrust his hand into his pocket, she stopped, expecting something. 'Diable!' exclaimed the poet, finding at the bottom of his pocket the reality, that is to say, nothing at all; the pretty girl standing before him all the while, looking at him with her large eyes, holding out her tambourine, and waiting. Gringoire perspired from every pore.

Fortunately an unexpected incident came to his aid.

'Wilt thou begone, thou Egyptian locust?' cried a harsh voice from the darkest corner of the Place.

The girl turned affrighted. This was not the voice of the bald-headed man; it was the voice of a woman – bigoted and malicious.

This cry, which frightened the gypsy, highly delighted a troop of children that were rambling about.

'It's the recluse of the Tour-Rolland,' cried they with uproarious bursts of laughter – 'it's the nun that's scolding. Hasn't she had her supper? Let's carry her something from the town buffet.'

And they all ran toward the Maison aux Piliers.

Gringoire had availed himself of this agitation of the dancer to disappear among the crowd. The shouts of the children reminded him that he too had not supped. He therefore hastened to the public buffet. But the little rogues had better legs than he, and when he arrived they had cleared the table. They had not even left one wretched cake at five sous the pound.

'Tis an unpleasant thing to go without one's dinner. 'Tis less gratifying still to go without one's supper, and not know where to sleep. Gringoire was at that point.

He was sinking more and more deeply into this melancholy reverie, when he was suddenly startled from it by the sound of a strange but very sweet song. It was the young gypsy singing.

Her voice had the same character as her dance and her beauty. There was a continued succession of harmonious notes, of swells, of unexpected cadences – then simple strains, interspersed with sharp and shrill notes – then soft undulations, which rose and fell like the bosom of the youthful songstress. The expression of her sweet face followed with singular flexibility every capricious variation of her song, from the wildest inspiration to the most chastened dignity.

Gringoire felt the tears come to his eyes. Yet above all her song breathed gaiety, and she seemed to warble, like a bird, from pure lightness of heart.

The moment was short.

The same female voice which had interrupted the gypsy's dance, now interrupted her song.

'Wilt thou be silent, thou infernal cricket?' it cried, still from the same dark corner of the Place.

The poor 'cricket' stopped short, and Gringoire clapped his hands over his ears.

'Oh!' he cried, 'thou cursed, broken-toothed saw, that comest to break the lyre!'

The rest of the bystanders murmured with him. 'The devil take the nun!' cried some of them. And the invisible disturber might have found cause to repent of her attacks upon the gypsy had not their attention been diverted at that moment by the procession of the Fools' Pope, which, after traversing many a street and square, was now pouring into the Place de Grève, with all its torches and all its clamor.

This procession, which our readers have seen take its departure from the Palace, had increased on the way, having enlisted all the ragamuffins, the unemployed thieves and idle scamps in Paris.

In the center of this latter crowd, the great officers of the brotherhood of Fools bore upon their shoulders a stretcher, more loaded with wax-tapers than the shrine of Sainte Geneviève in time of pestilence; and seated upon this stretcher shone, crosiered and mitred, the new Fools' Pope, the ringer of Notre-Dame, Quasimodo the hunchback.

It is not easy to give an idea of the expression of proud and beatific joy which the melancholy and hideous visage of Quasimodo had attained in the journey from the Palace to the Grève. It was the first thrill of vanity that he had ever experienced. He had hitherto experienced nothing but humiliation, disdain at his condition, and disgust for his person. So, deaf as he was, he nevertheless relished, like a true pope, the acclamations of that crowd whom he had hated because he felt himself hated by them.

However, that the new Pope of the Fools analyzed the feelings which he experienced, or those which he inspired, we can by no means presume. The mind that was lodged in that misshapen body, was necessarily itself incomplete and dull of hearing; so that what he felt at that moment was both vague and confused to him. Only, joy beamed through all, and pride predominated.

It was, therefore, not without surprise and alarm that all at once, at the moment when Quasimodo, in that state of semi-intoxication, passed triumphantly before the Maison aux Piliers, a man was seen to dart from the crowd, and, with an angry gesture, snatch from his hands the crosier of gilt wood, ensign of his mock papacy.

The person who had this temerity was the man with the bald head, who, the moment before, standing in the crowd that encircled the gypsy, had chilled the poor girl's blood with his words of menace and hatred. He was in ecclesiastical dress. The moment he rushed forth from the crowd he was recognized by Gringoire, who had not before observed him. 'What!' said he, with a cry of astonishment. 'Why, 'tis my master in Hermes, Dom Claude Frollo, the archdeacon! What the devil can he want with that one-eyed brute? He will be devoured!'

A cry of terror proceeded from the multitude. The formidable Quasimodo had leaped down from his seat; and the women turned away their eyes, that they might not see him tear the archdeacon to pieces.

He made one bound toward the priest, looked in his face, and then fell on his knees, before him.

The priest snatched his tiara from his head, broke his crosier, and rent his tinsel cope.

Quasimodo remained upon his knees, bowed down his head, and clasped his hands.

They then entered into a strange dialogue of signs and gestures, for neither of them uttered a word. The priest, erect, angry, threatening, imperious; Quasimodo prostrate, humble, suppliant. And yet it is certain that Quasimodo could have crushed the priest with his thumb.

At last the priest, roughly shaking Quasimodo's powerful shoulder, made him a sign to rise and follow.

Quasimodo rose accordingly.

Then the brotherhood of Fools, their first amazement having passed, offered to defend their pope, thus abruptly dethroned.

Quasimodo, placing himself before the priest, gave full play the muscles of his athletic fists, and regarded the assailants, gnashing his teeth like an angry tiger.

The priest resumed his sombre gravity, and making a sign to Quasimodo, withdrew in silence.

Quasimodo walked before him, scattering the crowd in his passage.

When they had made their way through the populace and across the Place, the crowd of the curious and idle wished to follow them. Quasimodo then placed himself in the rear, and followed the archdeacon backwards, looking squat, snarling, monstrous, shaggy, gathering up his limbs, licking his tusks, growling like a wild beast, and swaying backward the crowd by a mere glance or gesture.

At length they both disappeared down a gloomy narrow street, into which no one dared to follow them; so effectually was its entrance barred by the mere image of Quasimodo gnashing his teeth.

3

Gringoire had set himself to follow the gypsy girl at all hazards. He had seen her, with her goat, turn down the Rue de la Contellerie; and, accordingly, he turned into the Rue de la Contellerie likewise.

'Why not?' said he to himself.

As a practical philosopher of the streets of Paris, Gringoire had remarked that nothing is more favorable to a state of reverie than to follow a pretty woman without knowing whither she is going.

However, nothing better disposes a man for following people in the street (especially when they happen to be women), a thing Gringoire was always ready to do, than not knowing where to sleep.

He walked along, therefore, thoughtfully, behind the young girl, who quickened her step, making her pretty little four-footed companion trot beside her, as she saw the townsfolk reaching their homes and the taverns closing for the night.

'After all,' he half thought to himself, 'she must have a lodging somewhere – the gypsy women have good hearts – who knows?'

The streets were every moment becoming darker and more solitary. The curfew had long ceased to ring, and it was only at long intervals that a person passed along the pavement, or a light was seen at a window. Gringoire, in following the gypsy, had involved himself in that inextricable labyrinth of alleys, courts and crossings which surrounds the ancient sepulchre of the Holy Innocents, but through which the girl followed a track that seemed to be well known to her, and with a step of increasing rapidity.

For some moments past his step had attracted the girl's attention; she had several times turned her head towards him with uneasiness: once, indeed, she had stopped short, had availed herself of a ray of light that escaped from a half-open bakehouse, to survey him steadily from head to foot; then, after this scrutiny, Gringoire had observed on her face the little grimace which he had already remarked, and she had gone on without more ado.

This same little pout furnished Gringoire with a subject of reflection. There certainly was both disdain and mockery in that pretty grimace. And he was beginning to hang his head, to count the paving-stones, and to follow the girl at a rather greater distance; when, at the turn of a street which for a moment hid her from view, he heard her utter a piercing shriek.

He quickened his step.

The street was filled with deep shadows. Yet, a wick soaked in oil, which was burning in a sort of iron cage, at the foot of a statue of the Holy Virgin at the corner of the street, enabled Gringoire to discern the gypsy struggling in the arms of two men, who were endeavoring to stifle her cries, while the poor little goat, in great alarm, put down her horns, bleating.

'Hither! hither! gentlemen of the watch!' cried Gringoire; and he advanced bravely.

One of the men who had laid hold of the girl, turned toward him. It was the formidable visage of Quasimodo.

Gringoire did not fly – but he did not advance another step.

Quasimodo came up to him, and hurling him some four paces off upon the pavement with a backstroke of his hand, plunged rapidly into the darkness, bearing the girl, whose figure drooping over his arm was like a silken scarf. His companion followed him, and the poor goat ran behind with its plaintive bleat.

'Murder! Murder!' cried the unfortunate gypsy.

'Stand, there! you scoundrels! and let go the wench!' was all at once heard in a voice of thunder, from a horseman, who suddenly made his appearance from the neighboring crossway.

It was a captain of the king's archers, armed from head to foot with broadsword in hand.

He snatched the gypsy from the grasp of the amazed Quasimodo, laid her across his saddle, and, at the moment when the redoubtable hunchback, having recovered from his surprise, was rushing upon him to regain possession of his prey, fifteen or sixteen archers, who followed close upon their captain, made their appearance, each brandishing his two-edged blade.

Quasimodo was surrounded, seized and garroted. He roared, he foamed, he bit; and had it been daylight, no doubt his visage alone, rendered yet more hideous by rage, would have put the whole detachment to flight. But the darkness had disarmed him of his most formidable weapon, his ugliness.

His companion had disappeared during the struggle.

The gypsy gracefully gained her seat upon the officer's saddle, rested both her hands upon the young man's shoulders, and looked fixedly at him for a few seconds, as if delighted with his fine countenance and the effectual help he had rendered her.

Then speaking first, and making her sweet voice still sweeter, she said to him:

'Monsieur le gendarme, what is your name?'

'Captain Phœbus de Chateaupers, at your service, my fair one,' said the officer, drawing himself up.

'Thank you,' said she.

And while Captain Phœbus was curling his moustache, she glided down from the horse like an arrow falling to the ground, and fled.

A flash of lightning could not have vanished more quickly.

'By the Pope's head!' exclaimed the captain, while he tightened the bands upon Quasimodo, 'I'd rather have kept the wench.'

'What would you have, captain?' said one of the archers. 'The linnet is flown – the bat remains.'

4

Gringoire, quite stunned with his fall, lay stretched upon the pavement before the good Virgin at the corner of the street. By degrees, however, he recovered his senses. At first, he was for some minutes in a sort of half-somnolent reverie, which was not altogether disagreeable, and in which the airy figures of the gypsy and the goat were confounded in his imagination with the weight of Quasimodo's fist. This state of his feelings was of short duration. A very lively sense of cold upon that part of his body which was in contact with the pavement, suddenly awoke him, and brought his mind to the surface.

'The devil take the humpbacked cyclops!' grumbled he between his teeth, as he strove to get up. But he was too much stunned, and too much bruised; he was forced to remain where he was. Having, however, the free use of his hand, he stopped his nose, and resigned himself to his situation.

'The mud of Paris,' thought he, for he now believed it to be decided that the gutter was to be his lodging, 'the mud of Paris is particularly foul. It must contain a large proportion of volatile and nitrous salts.'

He was reminded of the Archdeacon Claude Frollo. He reflected on the scene of violence of which he had just had a glimpse; that he had seen the gypsy struggling between two men; that Quasimodo had a companion; and the sullen and haughty countenance of the archdeacon floated confusedly in his memory. 'That would be strange,' thought he; and then, with this data and upon this basis, he began to erect the fantastic framework of hypothesis; then suddenly returning once more to reality, 'Oh, I freeze!' he cried.

The position was in fact becoming less and less tenable. Each particle of water in the channel carried off a particle of warmth from the loins of Gringoire; and an equilibrium of temperature between his body and the water was beginning to establish itself in the most cruel manner.

5

He then began to retrace his steps, and ferreted about to discover where he was – but in vain. All was intersections of streets, courts and blind alleys, amongst which he incessantly doubted and hesitated. At length he lost patience, and vehemently exclaimed, 'A curse upon these crossroads! the devil himself has made them after the image of his pitchfork!'

This exclamation relieved him a little; and a sort of reddish reflection, which he at that moment perceived at the end of a long and narrow street, completed the restoration of his courage.

He had no sooner advanced a few paces down the long street or lane, which was on a declivity, unpaved, descending more abruptly and becoming more miry the farther he proceeded, than he observed something very unusual. The street was not deserted; here and there were to be seen crawling certain vague shapeless masses, all moving toward the light which was flickering at the end of the street.

Nothing makes a man so adventurous as an empty pocket. Gringoire went forward, and soon came up with that one of the larvae which seemed to be dragging itself along indolently after the others. On approaching it, he found that it was nothing other than a miserable cripple fixed in a bowl, without legs or thighs, jumping along with the aid of his two hands, like a mutilated spider, with only two of its feet remaining.

He came up to another of these ambulatory masses, and examined it. It was a cripple, both in arms and legs, after such a manner that the complicated system of crutches and wooden legs that supported him made him look like a perambulating mason's scaffolding.

This being saluted him as he went by; but staying his hat just at the height of Gringoire's chin, after the manner of a shaving dish, and shouting in his ears, '*Senor Cabarellero, para comprar un pedaso de pan!*' (Sir, Cavalier, something with which to buy a piece of bread!)

'It appears,' said Gringoire, 'that this one talks too; but it's a barbarous language, and he's more lucky than I if he understands it.' Then striking his forehead through a sudden transition of idea: 'Apropos! what the devil did they mean this morning with their Esmeralda?'

He resolved to double his pace; but for the third time something blocked up the way. This something, or rather this some-one, was a blind man, a little man, with a bearded Jewish face, who, rowing in the space about him with a stick, and towed along by a great dog, whined out to him with a Hungarian accent, '*Facitote caritatem!*' (Give alms.)

'My friend,' said he, turning to the blind man, 'a week since I sold my last shirt.'

This said, he turned his back upon the blind man and pursued his way. But the blind man lengthened his pace at the same time; and behold, also, the cripple and the stump came up in great haste, with much noise of the platter that carried the one, and the crutches that sustained the other. All three, tumbling over each other at the heels of poor Gringoire, and calling their several songs.

He began to run. The blind man ran. The wooden legs ran. The stump ran.

And then, as he hurried still farther down the street, stump men, wooden-legged men, and blind men came swarming around him – men with but a single hand, men with but one eye, lepers with their sores – issued from out houses, adjacent alleys, cellar-holes – howling, bellowing, yelping – all hobbling and clattering along, making their way toward the light, and wallowing in the mire like so many slugs after the rain.

Gringoire, still followed by his three persecutors, and not knowing what was to come of it all, walked on affrighted among the others, turning aside the limpers, striding over the stumpies, his feet entangled in that ant-hill of deformities.

The idea occurred to him to try to retrace his steps. But it was too late; all this army had closed upon his rear, and his three beggars held him. He went on, therefore, urged forward at once by that irresistible flood, by fear, and by a dizziness which made it all seem to him like a sort of horrible dream.

At last he reached the extremity of the street. It opened into an immense square, where a thousand scattered lights were wavering in the thick gloom of the night. Gringoire threw himself into it, hoping to escape by the speed of his legs from the three deformed spectres that had fixed themselves upon him.

'*Onde vas, hombre?*' (Whither goest, man?) cried the wooden legs, throwing aside his scaffolding, and running after him with as good a pair of legs as ever measured a geometrical pace upon the pavement of Paris.

Meanwhile the stumpy, erect upon his feet, clapped his heavy iron-sheathed platter over Gringoire's head, while the blind man stared him in the face with great flaming eyes.

'Where am I?' said the terrified poet.

'In the Court of Miracles,' answered a fourth spectre who had accosted them.

'On my soul,' returned Gringoire, 'I do indeed find here that the blind see and the lame walk – but where is the Saviour?'

They answered with a burst of laughter of a sinister kind.

The poor poet cast his eyes around him. He was in fact in that terrible Court of Miracles, where no honest man had ever penetrated at such an hour – a magic circle, in which officers and sergeants disappeared in morsels – the city of the thieves – a hideous wart on the face of Paris – a sink from whence escaped every morning, and to which returned to stagnate every night, that stream of vice, mendicity and vagrancy which ever flows through the streets of a capital – a monstrous hive, into which all the hornets of society returned each evening with their booty – a lying hospital, in which the gypsy, the unfrocked monk, the abandoned scholar covered with painted sores, beggars in the daytime, transformed themselves at night into robbers – in short, an immense cloak-room, in which dressed and undressed at that period all the actors in that everlasting drama which robbery, prostitution and murder enacted upon the pavements of Paris.

It was a large open space, irregular and illpaved, as was at that time every square in Paris. Fires, around which swarmed strange groups, were gleaming here and there. All was motion and clamor. There were shrieks of laughter, squalling of children and shrill voices of women. The arms and heads of this crowd cast a thousand fantastic gestures in dark outline upon the luminous background.

The weak and wavering rays that streamed from the fires enabled Gringore, amid his perturbation, to distinguish, all round the extensive enclosure, a hideous framing of old houses, the decayed, shriveled, and stooping fronts of which, pierced by one or two circular attic windows with lights behind them, seemed to him, in the dark, like enormous old women's heads, ranged in a circle, looking monstrous and crabbed, and winking upon the diabolical revels.

It was like a new world, unknown, unimagined, deformed, creeping, swarming, fantastic.

At that moment a distinct shout was raised from the buzzing

mob that surrounded him. 'Take him to the king! take him to the king!'

They dragged him along, each striving to fix his talons upon him. But the three beggars kept their hold, and tore him away from the others, vociferating, 'He is ours!'

The poet's frail doublet gave up the ghost in this struggle.

In crossing the horrible place his dizziness left him. After proceeding a few paces the feeling of reality returned. He began to adapt himself to the atmosphere of the place. In short, on examining the orgie more closely and with greater calmness, he dropped from the witches' sabbath to the tavern.

The Court of Miracles was, in truth, no other than a pothouse of thieves, but as red with blood as with wine.

The spectacle which presented itself to him when his tattered escort at length deposited him at his journey's end was little adapted to bring back his mind to poetry, though it were the poetry of hell. It was more than ever the prosaic and brutal reality of the tavern.

Round a large fire burning upon a great round flagstone, and the blaze of which had heated red-hot the legs of an iron trivet, empty for the moment, some worm-eaten tables were set out here and there in confusion. Upon these tables shone a few pots dripping with wine and beer, around which were grouped a number of bacchanalian visages, reddened by the fire and the wine. There would be a man with a fair round belly and a jovial face, noisily throwing his arms round a girl of the town, thick-set and brawny. Then a sort of false soldier who whistled away while he was undoing the bandages of his false wound, and unstiffening his sound and vigorous knees, which had been bound up since the morning in ample ligatures. Beyond him there was a mumper preparing, with suet and ox-blood, his sore legs, for the morrow. In another place a young scamp was taking a lesson in epilepsy from an old hustler, who was teaching him the art of foaming at the mouth by chewing a piece of soap; while four or five women thieves, just by them, were contending, at the same table, for the possession of a child stolen in the course of the evening.

Near the fire was a barrel, and upon the barrel was seated one of the beggars. This was the king upon his throne.

The three who held Gringoire brought him before this cask, and the whole bacchanalia were silent for a moment.

Gringoire dared not breathe nor raise his eyes.

But the king, from the top of his barrel, put the interrogatory, 'What is this knave?'

Gringoire started. This voice, though menacing in tone, reminded him of another voice which that very morning had struck the first blow at his mystery, by shouting out in the midst of the audience. He raised his eyes – it was indeed Clopin Trouillefou, whom he had seen that morning.

Clopin Trouillefou, arrayed in his regal ensigns, had not one rag more or less upon him. His sore on the arm had disappeared. In his hand he held one of those whips with lashes of whitleather, which were, at that time, used by the sergeants of the wand to drive back the crowd. He had upon his head a circular coif closed at the top; but it was difficult to distinguish whether it was a child's cushion or a king's crown, so similar are the two things.

However, Gringoire, without knowing why, had felt some revival of hope on recognizing in the king of the Court of Miracles the cursed beggar of the Grande Salle. 'Maître,' stammered he, ' – Monseigneur – Sire – How must I call you?' said he at last, having mounted to his utmost stretch of ascent, and neither knowing how to mount higher nor how to come down again.

'Monseigneur – Your Majesty – or Comrade – call me what you like, only despatch. What hast thou to say in thy defense?'

'In my defense!' thought Gringoire. 'That is unpleasant.' He replied, hesitating, 'I am he – he who this morning – '

'By the devil's claws!' interrupted Clopin, 'they name, rascal! and nothing more. Hark ye – thou art before three mighty sovereigns. We are thy judges. Thou has entered into the kingdom of Argot without being an Argotier – thou hast violated the privileges of our stronghold. Thou must be punished, unless thou art either a thief, a beggar, or a vagrant. Art thou anything of that sort? Justify thyself – tell over thy qualifications.'

'Alas!' said Gringoire, 'I have not that honor. I am the author – '

'That's enough,' interrupted Trouillefou; 'thou shalt be hanged. As you treat our people amongst you, so we treat yours amongst us. Such law as you mete to the Truands (vagbonds and outlaws) the Truands mete to you. It is but your fault if it be evil. 'Tis quite necessary that an honest man or two should now and then grin through the hempen collar – that makes the thing honorable. Come, friend, merrily share thy tatters among these young ladies. I'll have thee hanged for the amusement of the Truands, and thou shalt give them thy purse to drink thy health.'

This was a formidable harangue.

'Messeigneurs the emperors and kings!' said Gringoire coolly, 'you do not consider. My name is Pierre Gringoire – I am the poet whose morality was performed this morning in the Grande Salle of the Palace.'

'Ah! it is thee, master, is it? I was there, by God's head! Well, comrade, is it any reason, because thou tiredst us to death this morning, that thou shouldst not be hanged tonight?'

'I shall have trouble to get off,' thought Gringoire. However, he made another effort. 'I don't very well see,' said he, 'why the poets are not classed among the Truands. A vagrant! – why Æsopus was a vagrant. A beggar – Homer was a beggar. A thief – was not Mercurius a thief?'

Clopin interrupted him. 'Methinks,' said he, 'thou'st a mind to matagrabolize us with thy gibberish. *Pardieu!* Be hanged quietly, man; and don't make so much ado.' Trouillefou made a sign; whereupon the duke, and the emperor, came and ranged themselves about him in the form of a horseshoe, of which Gingoire, still roughly held, occupied the center. It was a semi-circle of rags, tatters and tinsel – of pitchforks and hatchets – of staggering legs and brawny arms – of sordid, dull and sottish faces. In the midst of this round table of beggary, Clopin Trouillefou, as the king of this peerage, dominated – in the first place, by the height of his cask – and then, by a certain haughty, savage and formidable air, which made his eyes flash, and corrected in his fierce profile the bestial type of the Truand race.

'Hark ye,' said he to Gringoire, while he caressed his shape-less chin with his horny hand, 'I don't see why thou shouldst not be hanged. To be sure, thou dost not seem to like it, and that's but natural – you burghers aren't used to it. You have exagger-ated its importance. After all, we don't wish thee any harm. There's one way of getting off for the moment. Wilt thou be one of us?'

One can imagine the effect this proposal produced upon Gringoire, who saw life about to escape him, and felt his grasp beginning to fail. He caught at it energetically.

'That I will – certainly, assuredly,' said he.

'I will just observe to thee,' resumed the king, 'that thou wilt be none the less hanged for all that.'

'The devil!' exclaimed the poet.

'Only,' continued Clopin, quite imperturbably, 'thou wilt be hanged later, with more ceremony, at the expense of the good city of Paris, upon a fine stone gibbet, and by honest men. That's some consolation.'

'Just so,' answered Gringoire.

'There are other advantages. As being a free burgher, thou wilt have to pay neither tax on the pavements, the lamps, nor for the poor; to which the burghers of Paris are subject.'

'Be it so,' said the poet; 'I consent. I am a Truand, an Argotier, a free burgher, a *petite flambe*, whatever you please.'

'It is not alone enough to be willing,' said Clopin, surlily. 'Goodwill doesn't put one onion more into the soup, and is of no use but for going to heaven – and there's a difference between heaven and Argot. To be received in Argot thou must prove that thou art good for something; and to do that thou must rummage the mannikin.'

'I will rummage anything you like,' said Gringoire.

Clopin made a sign; whereupon several Argotiers detached themselves from the circle, and returned a moment later. They brought two posts, terminated at the lower extremity by two wooden feet, which made them stand firmly on the ground. To the upper extremities of these posts they applied a crossbeam; the whole forming a very pretty portable gallows, which Gringoire had the satisfaction of seeing erected before him in the twinkling of an eye. Everything was there, including the rope, which gracefully depended from the transverse beam.

'What will be the end of all this?' thought Gringoire, with some uneasiness. But a noise of little bells which he heard at that moment put an end to his anxiety; it proceeded from a stuffed figure of a man which the Truands were suspending by the neck to the rope, a sort of scarecrow, clothed in red, and so completely covered with little bells and hollow jingling brasses, that there were enough to have harnessed thirty mules. These thousand miniature bells jingled for a time under the vibrations of the cord.

Then Clopin, pointing to an old tottering stool beneath the mannikin, said to Gringoire. 'Get upon that.'

Gringoire mounted upon the stool, and succeeded, not without some oscillations of his head and his arms, in recovering his balance.

'Now,' proceeded the king of Tunis, 'turn thy right foot round thy left leg, and rise on the toe of thy left foot.'

'Monseigneur,' said Gringoire, 'you are then absolutely determined that I shall break a limb!'

Clopin shook his head. 'Hark ye, friend,' said he, 'thou dost talk too much. It all amounts to this: thou must stand on tip-toe, then thou canst reach the mannikin's pocket, thrust in thy hand and pull out the purse concealed therein, and if thou dost all this without the sounding of a bell, well and good – thou shalt be a Truand. We shall then have nothing more to do but belabor thee soundly for a week.'

'Ventre-Dieu! I shall take good care,' said Gringoire. 'And if I make the bells jingle?'

'Then thou shalt be hanged. Dost thou understand?'

'Nay, I understand it not at all,' answered Gringoire.

'Hark ye once more. You're to put your hand in the mannikin's pocket and take out his purse. If one single bell stirs in the doing of it, you shall be hanged. Now dost understand?'

'Well,' said Gringoire, 'I understand that.'

'Come, hasten!' said the king, striking his barrel with his foot, which resounded like a big drum. 'Rifle the mannikin's pocket, and let's have done with it. I tell thee, once for all, that if I hear the smallest tinkle, thou shalt take the mannikin's place.'

The whole company of Argotiers applauded the words of Clopin, and ranged themselves in a circle round the gallows with so pitiless a laugh that Gringoire saw plainly enough that he gave them too much amusement not to have everything to fear. He had, therefore, no hope left but in the faint chance of succeeding in the terrible operation which was imposed upon him.

Finding that there was no respite, delay, or subterfuge whatsoever, he bravely set about the feat. He turned his right foot about his left leg, lifted himself on the toe of his left foot, and stretched out his arm; but the moment that he touched the manikin, his body, which was supported only by one foot, tottered upon the stool, which had only three, he mechanically caught at the mannikin, lost his balance and fell heavily to the ground, quite deafened by the fatal vibration of the scarecrow's thousand bells; while the figure, yielding to the impulse which his hand had given it, first revolved on his own axis, and then swung majestically backwards and forwards between the two posts.

'*Malédiction!*' he exclaimed as he fell; and he lay with his face to the ground as if he were dead.

However, he heard the diabolical laughter of the Truands and the voice of Trouillefou, saying, 'Lift the fellow up, and hang him promptly.'

He rose by himself. They had already unhooked the mannikin to make room for him.

The Argotiers made him get upon the stool again. Clopin came up to him, passed the rope round his neck, and, slapping him on the shoulder, 'Good-bye, friend,' said he; 'thou'lt not escape now, though thou shouldst have the digestion of the pope himself.'

But he stopped as if struck by a sudden idea. 'Wait a moment,' said he; 'I am forgetful. It is our custom not to hang a man without first asking if there be a woman who will have him. Comrade, it's thy last chance! thou must marry either a Truand or the halter.'

Gringoire took breath. This was the second time he had come to life within half an hour; so that he dared not be too confident.

'Hello!' shouted Clopin, who had reascended his cask: 'hello, there! women! females! is there among you all, from the witch to her cat, ever a jade that will have this rogue? A man for nothing! Who will have him?'

Gringoire, in this miserable plight, was, it may be supposed, not over-inviting. The women displayed no great enthusiasm at the proposal. The unhappy fellow heard them answer: 'No, no – hang him! it will amuse us all!'

'Comrade,' said Clopin, 'thou'rt unlucky.'

Then rising on his barrel, 'So nobody bids?' cried he, mimicking the tone of an auctioneer, to the great diversion of all – 'so nobody bids? Going – going – going – ' then turning toward the gallows with a motion of his head, 'gone.'

At that moment a cry was raised among the Argotiers, of 'La Esmeralda! La Esmeralda!'

Gringoire started, and turned toward the side from which the shout proceeded. The crowd opened and made way for a clear and dazzling figure.

It was the gypsy girl.

This fascinating creature seemed to exercise, even over the Court of Miracles, her sway of grace and beauty. Argotiers, male and female, drew up gently to let her pass by; and their brutal countenances softened at her look.

She approached the victim with her elastic step, her pretty Djali following her. Gringoire was more dead than alive. She gazed at him for a moment in silence.

'Are you going to hang this man?' said she gravely to Clopin.

'Yes, sister,' answered the king of Tunis, 'unless thou wilt take him for thy husband.'

She made her pretty little grimace with her under lip.

'I will take him,' she said.

Gringoire was firmly persuaded that he must have been in a dream ever since the morning, and that this was but a continuation of it.

They undid the noose, and let the poet descend from the stool. His agitation obliged him to sit down.

The duke of Egypt, without uttering a word, brought forth a clay pitcher. The gypsy girl presented it to Gringoire. 'Throw it on the ground,' said she.

The pitcher broke in four pieces.

'Brother,' said the duke of Egypt, laying his hands upon their foreheads, 'she is thy wife – sister, he is thy husband – for four years. Go your ways.'

In a few minutes our poet found himself in a little chamber with a Gothic-vaulted ceiling, very snug, very warm, seated before a table which seemed to ask nothing better than to borrow a few articles from a hanging cupboard near by; having a good bed in prospect, and alone with a pretty girl. The adventure partook of enchantment. He began seriously to take himself for the hero of a fairy-tale.

The girl seemed to pay no attention to him. She was going back and forth, shifting first one article and then another, chatted with her goat, repeating her little grimace every now and then. At length she came and sat down near the table, and Gringoire could contemplate her at leisure.

'This, then,' said he to himself, as his eyes vaguely followed her, 'is Esmeralda – a heavenly creature! – a dancer in the streets – so much, and yet so little! A pretty woman, upon my word! – and who must love me to distraction, to take me in this fashion. Now I think on't,' said he, suddenly rising up from his seat, with that feeling of the real which formed the substance of his character and of his philosophy, 'I know not quite how it is – but I am her husband!'

With this idea in his head, and in his eyes, he approached the young girl in so military and lover-like a manner that she drew back. 'What do you want?' she said.

'Can you ask, adorable Esmeralda?' replied Gringoire, in such impassioned tones that he himself was astonished at his own accents.

The gypsy opened her large eyes. 'I know not your meaning.'

'What!' rejoined Gringoire, growing more and more excited, and thinking that, after all, he was only dealing with the ready-made virtue of the Count of Miracles, 'am I not thine, sweet friend? – art thou not mine?'

And quite guilelessly he clasped her waist.

The girl's bodice slipped through his hands like the skin of an eel. She sprang from one end of the little cell to the other, stooped, and rose again with a small poniard in her hand, before Gringoire had time to see whence the dagger came – irritated and indignant, with swelling lips, dilated nostrils, cheeks red as crab apples, and her eyes flashing lightning. At the same time the little white goat placed itself before her, and presented a battle-front to Gringoire, bristling with two pretty gilded and very sharp horns. This was all done in the twinkling of an eye.

The damsel had turned wasp, with every disposition to sting.

Our philosopher stood crestfallen, looking confusedly, first at the goat and then at its mistress. 'Holy Virgin!' he exclaimed at last, as soon as his surprise permitted him to speak, 'here are two tricksters!'

The gypsy now broke silence. 'Thou must be a very bold rascal!' she said.

'Forgive me, mademoiselle,' said Gringoire, with a smile; 'but why did you marry me then?'

'Was I to let them hang thee?'

'So,' rejoined the poet, somewhat disappointed in his amorous expectations, 'you had no other intention in marrying me but to save me from the gibbet?'

'And what other intention dost think I could have had?'

'Mademoiselle Esmeralda,' said the poet, 'let us compromise. I swear to you, by my chance of salvation, that I will not approach you without your leave and permission. But pray, give me supper.'

The truth is, that Gringoire, was 'very little of a voluptuary'. He was not of that cavalier species who carry girls by assault. In a love affair, as in every other affair, he willingly resigned himself to temporizing and to middle terms; and a good supper, in comfortable tête-à-tête, appeared to him, especially when he was hungry, to be a very good interlude.

A moment later a rye loaf, a slice of bacon, some withered apples and a jug of beer were on the table. Gringoire set to with avidity. To hear the furious clatter of his iron fork upon his earthen-ware plate, it seemed as if all his love had turned to hunger.

The young girl, seated near him, looked on in silence, evidently preoccupied by some other thought, at which she smiled from time to time, while her delicate hand caressed the intelligent head of the goat, pressed softly against her knee.

A candle of yellow wax lighted this scene of voracity and reverie.

However, the first cravings of his stomach being appeased, Gringoire felt a twinge of shame at seeing that there was only an apple left.

'Mademoiselle Esmeralda,' said he, 'you do not eat.'

She answered by a negative motion of the head; and her pensive gaze seemed to fix itself upon the vaulted ceiling of the chamber.

'What the deuce is she thinking about?' thought Gringoire; 'it can not be that grinning dwarf's face carved upon that keystone, that attracts her so mightily. The devil's in it if I can not at least bear that comparison.'

He raised his voice – 'Mademoiselle.'

She seemed not to hear him.

He repeated, louder still, 'Mademoiselle Esmeralda!' It was in vain. The girl's mind was elsewhere, and Gringoire's voice had not the power to bring it back. Luckily, the goat interfered. She began to pull her mistress gently by the sleeve. 'What do you want, Djali?' said the gypsy, briskly, with a sudden start.

'She is hungry,' said Gringoire, delighted at an opportunity of entering into conversation.

La Esmeralda began to crumble some bread, which Djali nibbled daintily from the hollow of her hand.

Gringoire, however, allowed her no time to resume her reverie. He ventured a delicate question: 'You will not have me for your husband, then?'

The girl looked fixedly at him, and answered, 'No.'

'For your lover?' proceeded Gringoire.

She pouted, and again answered, 'No.'

'For your friend?' then demanded the poet.

Again she looked at him fixedly; and, after a moment's reflection, said, 'Perhaps.'

'What must one be then to please you?'

'He must be a man.'

'And I,' said he, 'what am I then?'

'A man has a helmet on his head, a sword in his hand and gilt spurs at his heels.'

'Good!' said Gringoire; 'the horse makes the man. Do you love anybody?'

'As a lover?'

'Yes – as a lover.'

She remained pensive a moment. Then she said, with a peculiar expression, 'I shall know soon.'

'Why not tonight?' rejoined the poet, in a tender tone. 'Why not me?'

She gave him a grave look, and said: 'I can not love a man who can not protect me.'

Gringoire colored and took the reflection to himself. The girl evidently alluded to the feeble assistance he had lent her in the critical situation in which she had found herself two hours before. This recollection, effaced by his other adventures of the evening, now returned to him. He struck his forehead. 'Apropos, mademoiselle,' said he, 'I ought to have begun with that – pardon my foolish distractions – how did you contrive to escape from the clutches of Quasimodo?'

At this question the gypsy started. 'Oh! the horrible hunchback!' said she, hiding her face in her hands, and she shivered as if icy cold.

'Horrible, indeed!' said Gringoire, still pursuing his idea. 'But how did you manage to escape him?'

La Esmeralda smiled, sighed and was silent.

'Do you know why he followed you?' asked Gringoire, striving to come round again to the object of his inquiry.

'I don't know,' said the girl. Then she added quickly, 'But you were following me also. Why did you follow me?'

'In good faith,' replied Gringoire, 'I do not know.'

There was a pause. Gringoire was marking the table with his knife. The girl smiled, and seemed to be looking at something through the wall.

'Why do they call you La Esmeralda?' asked the poet.

'I don't know at all.'

'But why do they?'

She drew from her bosom a small oblong bag, suspended from her neck by a chain of grains of adrez arach (sweet-scented gum). A strong smell of camphor exhaled from the bag; it was covered with green silk, and had in the centre a large piece of green glass in imitation of an emerald.

'Perhaps it's on account of that,' said she.

Gringoire offered to take the bag, but she drew back. 'Touch it not,' she said, ' 'tis an amulet. Thou wouldst do mischief to the charm, or the charm to thee.'

The poet's curiosity was more and more awakened. 'Who gave it you?' said he.

She placed her finger on her lips, and hid the amulet again in her bosom. She made her usual pretty grimace – 'I don't even know thy name.'

'My name? – You shall have it if you wish: Pierre Gringoire.'

'I know a finer one,' said she.

'Cruel girl!' rejoined the poet. 'No matter – you shall not provoke me. Nay, you will perhaps love me when you know me better.'

'Phœbus,' said she, in an undertone; then, turning to the poet, 'Phœbus,' said she, 'what does that mean?'

Gringoire, though not at all understanding what relation there could be between his address and this question, was not sorry to show his erudition. He answered, bridling with dignity, ' 'Tis a Latin word, that signifies the sun.'

'The sun!' repeated she.

' 'Tis the name of a certain handsome archer, who was a god,' added Gringoire.

'A god!' repeated the gypsy; and there was something pensive and impassioned in her tone.

At that moment, one of the bracelets came unfastened and fell. Gringoire eagerly stooped to pick it up; and when he rose again, the girl and the goat had both disappeared. He heard the sound of a bolt. It was a small door, communicating no doubt with an adjoining chamber, which was fastened on the other side.

'Has she, at least, left me a bed?' said our philosopher.

He made a tour of the chamber. There was no piece of furniture at all adapted to repose, except a very long wooden chest; and the lid of that was carved; so that it gave Gringoire, when he stretched himself upon it, a sensation much like that which Micromegas, of Voltaire's story, would experience, lying at full length upon the Alps.

BOOK THREE

1

Sixteen years previous to the period of this story, on a fine morning of the first Sunday after Easter – called in France, Quasimodo Sunday – a living creature had been laid, after mass, in the church of Notre-Dame, upon the wooden bed fastened into the pavement on the left hand. Upon the bed it was customary to expose foundlings to public charity; whoever cared to, took them. In front of the bed was a copper basin for alms.

The sort of living creature which lay upon that board on Quasimodo Sunday morning, in the year of our Lord 1467, appeared to excite, in a high degree, the curiosity of a very considerable group of persons which had gathered around the bed. It consisted, in great measure, of individuals of the fair sex. They were nearly all old women.

In the first row, and bending the farthest over the bed, were four, who appeared to be attached to some religious community.

'What ever can that be, sister?' said Agnès to Gauchère, as she looked at the little exposed creature, which lay yelping and wriggling upon the wooden bed, frightened at being looked at by so many people.

'What is to become of us,' said Jehanne, 'if that is the way children are made now?'

'I am not learned in the matter of children,' resumed Agnès, 'but it must surely be a sin to look at such a one as this!'

' 'Tis no child at all, Agnès.'

' 'Tis a misshapen baboon,' observed Gauchère. 'It should be burned.'

In fact, the 'little monster' was no new-born infant. It was a little, angular, restless mass, imprisoned in a canvas bag marked with the cipher of Messire Guillaume Chartier, then bishop of Paris – with a head coming out at one end. This head was a misshapen enough thing; there was nothing of it to be seen but a shock of red hair, one eye, a mouth and some teeth. The eye wept; the mouth bawled; and the teeth seemed only waiting a chance to bite. The whole lump was struggling violently in the bag, to the great wonderment of the increasing and incessantly renewing crowd around it.

For some moments a young priest had been listening to the arguments of the nuns. His was a severe countenance, with a broad forehead and a penetrating eye. He silently put aside the crowd, scrutinized the *little monster* and stretched out his hand over him.

'I adopt this child,' said the priest.

He wrapped it in his cassock, and bore it away; the bystanders looked after him with frightened glances. A moment later he disappeared through the Red Door, which then led from the church to the cloister.

When the first surprise was over, Jehanne de la Tarme whispered in the ear of La Gaultière:

'I always said to you, sister, that that young clerk, Monsieur Claude Frollo, was a sorcerer.'

2

Claude Frollo was in fact no common person.

He belonged to one of those families of middle rank called indifferently, in the impertinent language of the last century, high commoners or petty nobility.

Claude Frollo had, from infancy, been destined by his parents for the ecclesiastical state. He had been taught to read in Latin; he had been trained to cast down his eyes and to speak low. While yet a child, his father had cloistered him in the college of Torchi, in the University. There it was that he had grown up, on the missal and the lexicon.

He was, moreover, a melancholy, grave and serious boy, who studied ardently and learned quickly; he was never boisterous at play; he mixed little in the bacchanalia of the Rue du Fouarre.

He was possessed by an absolute fever for the acquiring and storing of knowledge. At eighteen, he had made his way through the four faculties; it seemed to the young man that life had but one sole aim: knowledge.

It was about this period that the excessive heat of the summer of 1466 gave birth to the great plague which carried off more than forty thousand souls within the viscounty of Paris. The rumor spread through the University that the Rue Tirechappe was especially devastated by the pestilence. It was there that the parents of Claude resided. The young scholar hastened in great alarm to his paternal mansion. On entering, he found that his father and mother had both died the preceding day. A baby brother, in swaddling clothes, was yet living, and lay crying abandoned in its cradle. It was all that remained to Claude of his family. The young man took the child under his arm, and went away thoughtfully. Hitherto, he had lived only in science; he was now beginning to live in the world.

This catastrophe was a crisis in Claude's existence. An orphan, the eldest head of the family at nineteen, he felt himself rudely aroused from scholastic reveries to the realities of this world. Then, moved with pity, he was seized with love and devotion for this infant, his brother; and strange at once and sweet was this human affection to him who had never yet loved anything but books.

This affection developed itself to a singular degree; in a soul so new to passion it was like a first love. Separated since childhood from his parents, whom he had scarcely known – cloistered and immured, as it were, in his books – eager above all things to study and to learn – the poor scholar had not yet had time to feel that he had a heart. This little brother, without father or mother – this little child which had fallen suddenly from heaven into his arms – made a new man of him. He found that man has need of affections; that life without tenderness and without love was but dry machinery, noisy and wearing. Only he fancied – for he was still at that age when illusions are replaced by illusions – that the affections of blood and kindred were the only ones necessary; and that a little brother to love sufficed to fill a whole existence.

He threw himself, then, into the love of his little Jehan, with all the intensity of a character already deep, ardent, concentrated. This poor, helpless creature, pretty, fair-haired, rosy and curly – this orphan with none to look to for support but another orphan – moved him to the inmost soul; and, serious thinker as he was, he began to reflect upon Jehan with a feeling of the tenderest pity. He cared for him and watched over him as over something very fragile and very precious; he was more than a brother to the infant – he became a mother to it.

Thenceforward, feeling that he had a burden to bear, he took life very seriously. The thought of his little brother became not only his recreation, but the object of his studies. He resolved to consecrate himself entirely to a future for which he made himself answerable before God, and never to have any other wife, nor any other child, than the happiness and prosperity of his brother. He accordingly became more than ever attached to his clerical vocation. His merit, his learning, his quality as an immediate vassal of the Bishop of Paris, threw the doors of the Church wide open to him. At twenty years of age, by special dispensation from the Holy See, he was ordained priest; and served, as the youngest of the chaplains of Notre-Dame, at the altar called, on account of the late mass that was said at it, *altare pigrorum*, the altar of the lazy.

There, more than ever buried in his dear books, which he only left to hasten for an hour to the fief Du Moulin, this mixture of learning and austerity, so rare at his age, had speedily gained him the admiration and respect of the cloister. From the cloister his reputation for learning had spread to the people, among whom it had been in some degree changed, as not unfrequently happened in those days, into reputation for sorcery.

Then it was that he had approached the unfortunate little creature, the object of so much hatred and menace. Its distress, its deformity, its abandonment, the thought of his little brother – the idea which suddenly crossed his mind that, were he to die, his dear little Jehan might also be cast miserably upon the board for foundlings – all this rushed into his heart at once – a deep feeling of pity had taken possession of him, and he had borne away the child.

When he took the child from the bag, he found it to be very deformed indeed. The poor little imp had a great wart covering its left eye – the head compressed between the shoulders – the spine crooked – the breastbone prominent – and the legs bowed. Yet it seemed to be full of life; and although it was impossible to discover what language it babbled, its cry proclaimed a certain degree of health and strength. Claude's compassion was increased by this ugliness; and he vowed in his heart to bring up this child for the love of his brother; in order that, whatever might be the future faults of little Jehan, there might be placed to his credit this piece of charity performed on his account. It was a sort of investment of good works in his little brother's name – a stock of good deeds which he wished to lay up for him beforehand – in case the little rascal should one day find himself short of that coin, the only kind taken at the toll-gate of Paradise.

He baptized his adopted child by the name of Quasimodo; whether it was that he chose thereby to mark the day upon which he had found him, or that he meant to characterize by that name how incomplete and imperfect the poor little creature was.

3

Now, in 1482, Quasimodo had grown up, and for several years had been ringer of the bells of Notre-Dame, thanks to his foster-father, Claude Frollo, who had become Archdeacon of Josas.

Quasimodo was, therefore, ringer of the chimes of Notre-Dame.

With time, a certain bond of intimacy had been established, uniting the bell-ringer to the church. Separated forever from the world by the double fatality of his unknown birth and his deformity – imprisoned from his infancy within that double and impassable circle – the poor wretch had been accustomed to see nothing of the world beyond the religious walls which had received him under their shadow. Notre-Dame had been to him, by turns, as he grew and developed, egg – nest – home – country – universe.

And it is certain that there was a mysterious harmony between this creature and the edifice. When, while yet quite little, he used to drag himself along, twisting and jerking, in the gloom of its arches, he seemed, with his human face and his bestial members, the native reptile of that damp, dark pavement.

And, later, the first time that he grasped mechanically the bell-rope in the towers, hung himself upon it and set the bell in motion, the effect upon Claude, his adoptive father, was that of a child whose tongue is loosed and who begins to talk.

Thus it was that his being, gradually unfolding, took its mould from the cathedral – living there – sleeping there – scarcely ever going out of it – receiving every hour its mysterious impress – he came at length to resemble it, to be fashioned like it, to make an integral part of it. His salient angles fitted themselves (if we may be allowed the expression) into the retreating angles of the edifice, and he seemed to be not only its inhabitant, but even the natural tenant of it. He might almost be said to have taken its form, as the snail takes that of its shell. It was his dwelling-place – his hole – his envelope.

It was his own particular dwelling-place. It had no depths which Quasimodo had not penetrated, no heights which he had not scaled. Many a time had he clambered up its front, one story after another, with no other aid than the projecting bits of carving; the towers, over the exterior of which he was frequently seen crawling like a lizard gliding upon an upright wall – those twin giants – so lofty, so threatening, so formidable – had for him neither vertigo, fright, nor sudden giddiness. So gentle did they appear under his hand, so easy to scale, one would have said that he had tamed them.

Moreover, not only his body, but also his mind, seemed to be moulded by the cathedral. Quasimodo was born one-eyed, hump-backed, limping. It was with great difficulty and great patience that Claude Frollo had taught him to speak. But a fatality pursued the poor foundling. Bell-ringer of Notre-Dame at fourteen years of age, a fresh infirmity had come to complete

43

his desolation – the sound of the bells had broken the drum of the ear; he had become deaf. The only door that nature had left wide open between him and the external world, had been suddenly closed forever.

In closing, it intercepted the sole ray of joy and light that still penetrated to the soul of Quasimodo. That soul was now wrapped in profound darkness. The poor creature's melancholy became as incurable and as complete as his deformity; added to which, his deafness rendered him in some sort dumb. For, that he might not be laughed at by others, from the moment that he realized his deafness, he determined resolutely to observe a silence which he scarcely ever broke, except when alone. He voluntarily tied up that tongue which Claude Frollo had worked so hard to set free. And hence it was that, when necessity compelled him to speak, his tongue was heavy and awkward, like a door the hinges of which have grown rusty.

If now we were to endeavor to penetrate through this thick and obdurate bark to the soul of Quasimodo – could we sound the depths of that ill-informed organization – were it possible for us to look, with a torch, behind these untransparent organs – to explore the darksome interior of that opaque being – to illumine its obscure corners and absurd blind-alleys doubtless we should find the poor creature in some posture of decrepitude, stunted and rickety – like those prisoners who grow old under the Leads of Venice, bent double in a stone chest too low and too short for them either to stand or to lie at full length.

The first effect of this fatal organization was to disturb the view which he took of external objects. He received from them scarcely any immediate perception. The external world seemed to him much farther off than it does to us.

The second effect of his misfortune was to render him mischievous.

He was mischievous, indeed, because he was savage; and he was savage because he was deformed. There was a logic in his nature as in ours.

We must, nevertheless, do him justice; malice was probably not innate in him. From his very first intercourse with men he had felt, and then had seen, himself repulsed, branded, despised. As he grew up, he had found around him nothing but hatred. What wonder that he should have caught it! He had contracted it – he had but picked up the weapon that had wounded him.

That which he loved above all in the maternal edifice – that which awakened his soul, and made it stretch forth its poor pinions, that otherwise remained so miserably folded up in its cavern – that which even sometimes made him happy – was, the bells. He loved them, caressed them, talked to them, understood

44

them. From the chimes in the central steeple to the great bell over the doorway, they all shared his affections. The belfry of the transept and the two towers were to him three great cages, in which the birds taught by himself sang for him alone. It was, however, those same bells that had deafened him.

It is impossible to form a conception of his joy on the days of the great peals. The instant the archdeacon let him off with the word 'go', he ascended the spiral staircase quicker than any other person could have gone down. He rushed, breathless, into the aërial chamber of the great bell; gazed at her for a moment attentively and lovingly; then began to talk to her softly; patted her with his hand, like a good horse setting out on a long journey. He pitied her for the labor she was about to undergo. After these first caresses, he called out to his assistants, placed in the lower story of the tower, to begin. The latter then hung their weight upon the ropes, the windlass creaked and the enormous cone of metal moved slowly. Quasimodo, with heaving breast, followed it with his eye. The first stroke of the tongue against the brazen wall that encircled it shook the scaffolding upon which he stood. Quasimodo vibrated with the bell. 'Vah!' he would cry, with a mad burst of laughter. Meanwhile, the motion of the bell was accelerated; and as it went on, taking an ever-increasing sweep, Quasimodo's eye, in like manner, opened more and more widely, phosphorescent and flaming. At length the grand peal began – the whole tower trembled – rafters, leads, stones – all shook together – from the piles of the foundation to the trefoils of the parapet. Then Quasimodo boiled and frothed; he ran to and fro, trembling, with the tower, from head to foot. The bell, let loose, and in a frenzy, turned first to one side and then to the other side of the tower its brazen throat, from whence issued a roar that was audible at four league's distance. Quasimodo placed himself before this gaping throat – he crouched down and rose with the oscillations of the bell – inhaled that furious breath – looked by turns down upon the Place which was swarming with people two hundred feet below him, and upon the enormous brazen tongue which came, second after second, to bellow in his ear. This was the only speech that he could hear, the only sound that broke for him the universal silence. He expanded in it, like a bird in the sunshine. All at once the frenzy of the bell would seize him; his look became wild – he lay in wait for the great bell as a spider for a fly, and then flung himself headlong upon it. Now, suspended over the abyss, borne to and fro by the formidable swinging of the bell, he seized the brazen monster by the ears – gripped it with his knees – spurred it with his heels – and redoubled, with the shock and weight of his body, the fury of the peal. Meanwhile, the tower trembled; he shouted and gnashed his teeth – his red hair bristled – his breast heaved and puffed like the bellows of a forge – his eye flashed fire – the monstrous bell neighed panting beneath him. Then it was no longer either the great bell of Notre-Dame, nor Quasimodo – it was a dream – a whirl – a tempest – dizziness astride upon clamor – a strange centaur, half man, half bell.

The presence of this extraordinary being seemed to infuse the breath of life into the whole cathedral. There seemed to issue from him – at least according to the growing superstitions of the crowd – a mysterious emanation, which animated all the stones of Notre-Dame, and to make the very entrails of the old church heave and palpitate. To know that he was there was enough to make one think the thousand statues in the galleries and door-ways moved and breathed. The old cathedral seemed to be a docile and obedient creature in his hands; waiting his will to lift up her mighty voice; being filled and possessed with Quasimodo as with a familiar spirit. One would have said that he made the immense building breathe. He was everywhere; he multiplied himself upon every point of the structure. Sometimes one beheld with dread, at the very top of one of the towers, a fantastic dwarfish-looking figure – climbing – twisting – crawling on all fours – descending outside over the abyss – leaping from projection to projection – and diving to ransack the belly of some sculptured gorgon; it was Quasimodo dislodging the crows. Again, in some obscure corner of the church, one would stumble against a sort of living chimera, crouching and scowling – it was Quasimodo musing. Sometimes one caught sight, under a belfry, of an enormous head and a bundle of ill-adjusted limbs, swinging furiously at the end of a rope – it was Quasimodo ringing the vespers, or the angelus. Often, at night, a hideous form was seen wandering upon the frail open-work balustrade which crowns the towers and runs around the top of the apse – it was still the hunchback of Notre-Dame. Then, so said the good women of the neighborhood, the whole church assumed a fantastic, supernatural, horrible aspect – eyes and mouths opened in it here and there – the dogs, and the dragons and the griffins of stone, that watch day and night, with outstretched necks and open jaws, around the monstrous cathedral, were heard to bark. And if it was a Christmas eve – while the big bell, that seemed to rattle in its throat, called the faithful to the blazing midnight mass, the gloomy façade assumed such an aspect that the great doorway seemed to swallow the multitude, while the rose-window above it looked on – and all this came from Quasimodo. Egypt would have taken him for the god of this temple – the Middle Ages believed him to be its demon – he was its soul.

So much so that, to those who know that Quasimodo once

46

existed, Notre-Dame is now deserted, inanimate, dead. They feel that something has disappeared. That vast body is empty – it is a skeleton – the spirit has quitted it – they see its place and that is all. It is like a skull, which still has holes for the eyes, but no longer sight.

4

There was, however, one human creature whom Quasimodo excepted from his malice and hatred for others, and whom he loved as much, perhaps more, than his cathedral: this was Claude Frollo.

The case was simple enough. Claude Frollo had taken him, adopted him, fed him, brought him up. While yet quite little, it was between Claude Frollo's knees that he had been accustomed to take refuge when the dogs and the children ran yelping after him. Claude Frollo had taught him to speak, to read, to write. Claude Frollo had made him ringer of the bells.

Accordingly, Quasimodo's gratitude was deep, ardent, boundless; and although the countenance of his adoptive father was often clouded and severe – although his mode of speaking was habitually brief, harsh, imperious – never had that gratitude wavered for a single instant. The archdeacon had in Quasimodo the most submissive of slaves, the most tractable of servants, the most vigilant of watch-dogs. When the poor bell-ringer became deaf, between him and Claude Frollo was established a language of signs, mysterious and intelligible only to themselves. Thus the archdeacon was the only human being with whom Quasimodo had preserved a communication. He had intercourse with only two things in this world – Notre-Dame and Claude Frollo.

Unexampled were the sway of the archdeacon over the bell-ringer, and the bell-ringer's devotion to the archdeacon. One sign from Claude, and the idea of pleasing him would have sufficed to make Quasimodo throw himself from the top of the towers of Notre-Dame. There was something remarkable in all that physical strength, so extraordinarily developed in Quasimodo, and blindly placed by him at the disposal of another. In this there was undoubtedly filial devotion and domestic attachment; but there was also fascination of one mind by another mind. There was a poor, awkward, clumsy organization, which stood with lowered head and supplicating eyes before a lofty and profound, a powerful and commanding intellect. Lastly, and above all, it was gratitude – gratitude pushed to its extremest

47

limit, that we know not to what to compare it. This virtue is not one of those of which the finest examples are to be met with among men. We will say, then, that Quasimodo loved the archdeacon as no dog, no horse, no elephant ever loved his master.

5

In 1482, Quasimodo was about twenty years old, and Claude Frollo about thirty-six. The one had grown up; the other had grown old.

Claude Frollo was no longer the simple student of the Torchi college – the young dreaming philosopher, who knew many things and was ignorant of many. He was a priest, austere, grave, morose.

Dom Claude Frollo, however, had abandoned neither science nor the education of his young brother, those two occupations of his life. But in the course of time, some bitterness had been mingled with these things once so sweet. Little Jehan Frollo, surnamed Du Moulin (of the mill) from the place where he had been nursed, had not grown up in the direction which Claude had been desirous of leading him. The elder brother had reckoned upon a pious, docile, studious, creditable pupil. But the younger brother was a very devil – very unruly – which made Dom Claude knit his brows – but very droll and very shrewd – which made the big brother smile.

Claude had consigned him to the same college de Torchi where he had passed his early years in study and meditation; and it grieved him that this sanctuary, once edified by the name of Frollo, should now be scandalized by it. He sometimes read Jehan very long and very severe lectures upon the subject, which the latter bore undaunted. After all the young scapegrace had a good heart – as is always the case in all comedies. But the lecture over, he nevertheless quietly resumed his dissolute and turbulent ways.

Owing to all this, Claude, saddened and discouraged in his human affections, had thrown himself the more eagerly into the arms of Science. He became more and more learned – and, at the same time, by a natural consequence, more and more rigid as a priest, more and more gloomy as a man.

As Claude Frollo had, from his youth, gone through almost the entire circle of human knowledge, positive, external and lawful, he was under the absolute necessity, of going farther, and seeking other food for the insatiable activity of his intellect.

Many grave persons affirmed that after exhausting the lawful in human knowledge he had dared to penetrate into the unlawful. He had, they said, successively tasted every apple upon the tree of knowledge; and, whether from hunger or disgust, he had ended by tasting the forbidden fruit. He had delved deeper — underneath all that finite, material, limited science; he had perhaps risked his soul, and seated himself in the cavern, at that mysterious table of the alchemists, the astrologers, the hermetics.

This is, as least, what was supposed, whether rightly or not.

It is certain that the archdeacon had been seized with a singular passion for the symbolical doorway of Notre-Dame.

Furthermore, it is certain that the archdeacon had established himself in a small and secret cell, into which no one entered — not even the bishop, it was said — without his leave. This cell, contrived of old, almost at the top of the tower, among the crows' nests, by Bishop Hugo de Besançon who had practised sorcery there in his day. What this cell contained no one knew. But from the strand of the Terrain there was often seen, at night, to appear, disappear and reappear, at short and regular intervals, at a small dormer window at the back of the tower, a certain red, intermittent, singular glow, seeming as if it followed the irregular puffing of a bellows, and as if proceeding from a flame rather than a light. In the darkness, at that height, it had a very weird appearance; and the housewives would say: 'There is the archdeacon blowing! Hell is making sparks up there!'

There were not, after all, any great proofs of sorcery; but still there was quite enough smoke to make the good people suppose a flame; and the archdeacon had a somewhat formidable reputation. We are bound to declare, however, that the science of Egypt — that necromancy — that magic — even the clearest and most innocent — had no more violent enemy, no more merciless denouncer before the officials of Notre-Dame, than himself. Whether it was sincere abhorrence, or merely the trick of the robber who cries Stop, thief! this did not prevent the archdeacon from being considered by the wise heads of the chapter as one who risked his soul upon the threshold of hell — one lost in the caverns of the cabala — groping his way among the shadows of the occult sciences. Neither were the people deceived thereby; to the mind of any one possessed of the least sagacity, Quasimodo passed for the demon, and Claude Frollo the sorcerer; it was evident that the bell-ringer was to serve the archdeacon for a given time, at the expiration of which he was to carry off the latter's soul by way of payment. Thus the archdeacon, despite the excessive austerity of his life, was in bad odor with all pious souls; and there was no devout nose, however inexperienced, but could smell him out for a magician.

And if, as he grew older, he had formed to himself abysses in science, others had likewise opened themselves in his heart. So at least they were led to believe who narrowly observed that face, in which his soul shone forth as through a sombre cloud. Whence that large bald brow – that head constantly bowed – that breast forever heaved with sighs? What secret thought wreathed that bitter smile about his lips, at the same instant when his lowering brows approached each other fierce as two encountering bulls? Why were his remaining hairs already gray? What internal fire was that which shone forth occasionally in his glance, to such a degree that his eye resembled a hole pierced in the wall of a furnace?

These symptoms of a violent moral preoccupation had acquired an especially high degree of intensity at the period to which our narrative refers.

However, he became doubly rigid, and had never been more exemplary. By character, as well as by calling, he had always held himself aloof from women; and he seemed to hate them more than ever. The mere crackling of a silken corsage brought his hood down over his eyes.

It was also remarked that, for some time past, his abhorrence of gypsy women and zingari had been redoubled. He had solicited from the bishop an edict expressly forbidding the gypsies from coming to dance and play upon the tambourine in the *Place du Parvis*; and for the same length of time he had been rummaging among the mouldy archives of the official in order to collect together all the cases of wizards and witches condemned to the flames or the halter for having been accomplices in sorcery with he-goats, she-goats or sows.

6

The archdeacon and the bell-ringer, as we have already said, were but little esteemed among the small and great folks of the environs of the cathedral. When Claude and Quasimodo went forth together, as frequently happened, and they were observed in company traversing the clean, but narrow and dusky, streets of the neighborhood of Notre-Dame, the servant following his master, more than one malicious word, more than one ironical couplet, more than one insulting jest, stung them on their way; unless Claude Frollo – though this happened rarely – walked with head erect, exhibiting his stern and almost august brow to the gaze of the abashed scoffers.

BOOK FOUR

1

A very fortunate personage, in 1482, was nobleman Robert d'Estouteville. Not only had he his particular court as provost and viscount of Paris, but also he had a share, both by presence and action, in the grand justice of the king. There was not a head of any distinction but passed through his hands before it fell into those of the executioner.

It was the day after the holiday when he was to hold a sitting in the Grand Châtelet.

However, the audience had begun without him. His deputies, civil, criminal and private, were acting for him, according to custom; and since the hour of eight in the morning, some scores of citizens, men and women, crowded and crammed into a dark corner of the lower courtroom of the Châtelet, between the wall and a strong barrier of oak, were blissfully looking on at the varied and exhilarating spectacle of the administration of civil and criminal justice by Maître Florian Barbedienne, auditor at the Châtelet, deputy of monsieur the provost, in a somewhat confused and utterly haphazard manner.

Now, the auditor was deaf. A slight defect for an auditor. Maître Florian delivered judgment, none the less, without appeal and quite competently. It is certainly quite sufficient that a judge should appear to listen; and the venerable auditor the better fulfilled this condition, the only one essential to strict justice, as his attention could not possibly be distracted by any noise.

And it was Quasimodo, bound, girded, roped, pinioned and well guarded who was to be tried that day. The detachment of sergeants that surrounded him were accompanied by the knight of the watch, in person, bearing the arms of France embroidered on his breast, and those of the Town on his back. There was nothing, however, about Quasimodo, excepting his deformity, to justify all this display of halberts and arquebusses. He was gloomy, silent and tranquil; only now and then did his single eye cast a sly and wrathful glance upon the bonds which confined him.

Meanwhile, Maître Florian, the auditor, turned over attentively the document in the complaint entered against Quasimodo, which the clerk handed him, and having glanced at it, appeared to reflect for a moment. Thanks to this precaution, which he was always careful to take at the moment of proceeding to an interrogatory, he knew beforhand the name, titles and misdeeds of the accused, made premeditated replies to answers foreseen; and so contrived to extricate himself from all the sinuosities of the interrogatory without too much exposing his deafness.

Having, then, well ruminated on the affair of Quasimodo, he threw back his head and half closed his eyes, by way of greater majesty and impartiality; so that, at that moment, he was blind as well as deaf – a double condition, without which no judge is perfect. It was in this magisterial attitude that he commenced the interrogatory:

'Your name?'

Quasimodo, receiving no intimation of the question thus addressed to him, continued to look fixedly at the judge, and made no reply. The deaf judge, receiving no intimation of the deafness of the accused, thought that he had answered, as accused persons generally did; and continued, with his mechanical and stupid self-confidence:

'Very well – your age?'

Again Quasimodo made no answer to this question. The judge, thinking it replied to, went on:

'Now – your calling?'

Still the same silence. The bystanders, however, were beginning to whisper and to exchange glances.

'Enough!' added the imperturbable auditor, when he supposed that the accused had finished his third reply. 'You are accused before us – firstly, with nocturnal disturbance; secondly, with dishonest violence upon the person of a foolish woman; thirdly, of rebellion and disloyalty toward the archers of the guard of our lord the king. Explain yourself on all these points. Clerk, have you taken down what the prisoner has said thus far?'

At this unlucky question a burst of laughter rose from both clerk and audience – so violent, so uncontrollable, so contagious, so universal, that neither of the deaf men could help perceiving it. Quasimodo turned round, shrugging his hump with disdain; while Maître Florian, equally astonished, and supposing that the laughter of the spectators had been excited by some irreverent reply from the accused, rendered visible to him by that shrug, apostrophized him indignantly.

'For that answer, fellow, you deserve the halter. Know you to whom you speak?'

This sally was not likely to check the explosion of the general mirth. It seemed to all present so incongruous and whimsical, that the wild laughter spread to the very sergeants of the Parloir aux Bourgeois, a sort of pikemen, whose stupidity was part of their uniform. Quasimodo alone preserved his gravity; for the very good reason that he understood nothing of what was going on around him. The judge, more and more irritated, felt obliged to proceed in the same strain, hoping thereby to strike the accused with a terror that would react upon the by-standers, and bring them back to a proper sense of respect:

'So, this is as much as to say, perverse and thieving knave that you are, that you presume to be lacking in respect to the auditor of the Châtelet; to the magistrate in charge of the chief police courts of Paris; appointed to inquire into all crimes, offenses and misdemeanors; to control all trades and prevent monopoly; to repair the pavements; to put d___n hucksters of poultry, fowl and wild game; to superin___ the measuring of firewood and other sorts of wood ...'

There is no reason why a deaf man talking to a deaf man should ever stop. Heaven knows where and when Maître Florian would have landed, thus launched at full speed in lofty eloquence, if the low door behind him had not suddenly opened and given entrance to monsieur the provost in person.

Maître Florian did not stop short at his entrance, but, turning half round upon his heel, and abruptly directing to the provost the harangue with which, a moment before, he was overwhelming Quasimodo:

'Monseigneur,' said he, 'I demand such penalty as it shall please you upon the accused here present, for flagrant and aggravated contempt of court.'

And he seated himself, utterly breathless, wiping away the great drops of sweat that fell from his brow and moistened, like tears, the parchments spread out before him. Messire Robert d'Estouteville frowned, and made a gesture to Quasimodo to attend, in a manner so imperious and significant that the deaf one in some degree understood it.

The provost addressed him sternly: 'What hast thou done to be brought hither, varlet?'

The poor devil, supposing that the provost was asking his name, broke the silence which he habitually kept, and in a harsh and guttural voice, replied – 'Quasimodo.'

The answer matched the question so little that the loud laugh began to circulate once more; and Messire Robert cried out, red with wrath: 'Dost mock me too, thou arrant knave?'

'Bell-ringer of Notre-Dame,' answered Quasimodo, thinking himself called upon to explain to the judge who he was.

'Bell-ringer, indeed! I'll make them ring a peal of rods on thy back through every street in Paris – dost thou hear, rascal?'

'If you want to know my age,' said Quasimodo, 'I believe I shall be twenty next Martinmas.'

This was too much. The provost could endure it no longer.

'Ha! so you jeer at the provostry, you wretch! Messieurs the sergeants of the wand, you will take me this knave to the pillory in the Grève, and there flog him and turn him for an hour. He shall pay for his impudence, 'Sdeath! And I order that this present sentence be proclaimed by four sworn trumpeters, in the seven castellanies of the viscounty of Paris.'

The clerk instantly fell to work to record the sentence.

However, at the moment when Maître Florian Barbedienne was in his turn reading over the judgement before signing it, the registrar felt himself moved with pity for the poor condemned wretch; and, in the hope of obtaining some mitigation of the penalty, he approached the auditor's ear as close as he could, and said, pointing to Quasimodo: 'That man is deaf.'

He hoped that a sense of their common infirmity would awaken Maître Florian's interest in behalf of the condemned. But, in the first place, as we have already observed, Maître Florian did not care to have his deafness remarked; in the next place, he was so hard of hearing that he did not catch a single word of what the clerk said to him; nevertheless, he wished to appear to have heard, and replied: 'Ah! ah! that is different – I did not know that. An hour more of the pillory, in that case.'

And he signed the sentence thus modified.

2

With the reader's permission we shall conduct him back to the Place de Grève, which we quitted yesterday with Gringoire, to follow La Esmeralda.

It is ten in the morning. The appearance of everything indicates the day after a festival. The pavement is strewn with rubbish, ribbons, rags, feathers from tufts of plumes, drops of wax from the torches and fragments from the public banquet. A good many of the townspeople loiter about – turning over with their feet the extinct brands of the bonfire – going into raptures before the Maison aux Piliers at the recollection of the fine hangings of the preceding day, and now contemplating the nails that fastened them, the only remnant of the ravishing spectacle.

Now, if the reader will, after surveying this lively and noisy scene which is being enacted in all parts of the square, turn his eyes toward that ancient half-Gothic, half-Roman building, the

Tour Roland, which stands at the western corner next the quay, he will observe, at the angle of its façade, a large public breviary richly illuminated, protected from the rain by a small penthouse, and from thieves by a grating, which, however, permits of the leaves being turned. Close by this breviary is a narrow, arched window-hole, guarded by two iron bars placed crosswise, and looking toward the square – the only opening through which a little air and light are admitted into a small cell without a door, built on the ground-floor, in the thickness of the wall of the old house – and filled with a stillness the more profound, a silence the more dead, inasmuch as a public square, the most populous and the noisiest in Paris, is swarming and clamoring around it.

This sort of tomb was not so very rare a thing in the cities of the Middle Ages. There might often be found, in the most frequented street, in the most crowded and noisy market-place – a walled and grated cabin – within which a human being prayed day and night, voluntarily devoted to some everlasting lamentation or some great expiation. A sort of intermediary link between the house and the tombs, the city and the cemetery.

To confine ourselves here to the cell in Roland's Tower – we are bound to declare that it had scarcely ever lacked for recluses. Since Madame Roland's death, it had rarely been vacant even for a year or two. Many a woman had come and mourned until death over the memory of her parent, her lover, or her failings.

There had been carved, also in large Roman capitals, over the window, these two words:

TU, ORA (Pray, thou).

Hence the people gave to this dark, damp, dismal cavity the name of *Trou aux Rats* or rat-hole.

3

At the time of which this story treats the cell in the Tour Roland was occupied. If the reader wishes to know by whom, he has but to listen to the conversation of three fair gossips, who, at the moment that we have called his attention to the Rat-Hole, were proceeding toward the same spot, going up the river-side from the Châtelet toward the Grève.

The first two walked with the step peculiar to Parisian women showing Paris to their country friends. The provincial one held by the hand a big, chubby boy, who held in his a large, flat cake.

The three damoiselles were all talking at once.

'Let us make haste, Damoiselle Mahiette,' said the youngest, who was also the lustiest of the three, to her country friend. 'I am much afraid we shall be too late; we were told at the Châtelet that they were to put him in the pillory forthwith.'

And Mahiette suddenly exclaimed. 'See those people, crowding together at the end of the bridge! There's something in the midst of them that they are looking at.'

'Surely I hear the sound of a tambourine,' said Gervaise. 'I think it's little Smeralda, doing her mummeries with her goat. Quick, Mahiette – make haste, and pull your boy along. You are come here to see the curiosities of Paris. Yesterday you saw the Flemings – today you must see the little gypsy.'

'The gypsy?' exclaimed Mahiette, turning sharply round and grasping tightly the arm of her son. 'God forbid! She would steal my child – Come, Eustache!'

And she set off running along the quay toward the Grève, until she had left the bridge far behind her. But the boy, whom she dragged after her, stumbled and fell upon his knees; she stopped out of breath. Oudarde and Gervaise now came up with her.

'That gypsy steal your child!' said Gervaise; 'that's an odd notion of yours!'

Mahiette shook her head thoughtfully.

' 'Tis singular,' observed Oudarde, 'that the Sachette has the same notion about gypsy women.'

'What's the Sachette?' inquired Mahiette.

'Hey!' said Oudarde, 'Sister Gudule.'

'And what is Sister Gudule?' returned Mahiette.

'She is the recluse of the Rat-Hole.' answered Oudarde.

'What?' asked Mahiette; 'the poor woman to whom we are carrying the cake?'

Oudarde nodded affirmatively.

'Just so. You will see her presently, at her window on the Grève. She looks as you do upon those vagabonds of Egypt who go about tambourining and fortune-telling. Nobody knows what has given her this horror of zingari and Egyptians. But you, Mahiette, wherefore should you take to your heels thus at the mere sight of them?'

'Oh!' said Mahiette, clasping with both hands the chubby head of her boy; 'I would not have that happen to me which happened to Pâquette la Chantefleurie!'

'Ah! you must tell us that story, good Mahiette,' said Gervaise, taking her arm.

'I will gladly,' answered Mahiette; 'but you must, indeed, be from Paris – not to know that! Pâquette la Chantefleurie's father died while Pâquette was quite a child, so she had only her mother. The two lived at Rheims, by the river-side, Rue de Folle Peine. Pâquette was so gay and so pretty, that everywhere they called her La Chantefleurie (the song blossom). Poor girl! What beautiful teeth she had! and she would laugh that she might show them. Now a girl who likes to laugh is on the high-road to weep – fine teeth are the ruin of fine eyes. Such was La Chantefleurie. She and her mother had hard work to earn their bread, their needlework brought them scarce more than six deniers a week, which is not quite two eagle farthings. One winter when the two women had no logs, the weather was very cold, and gave such a beautiful color to La Chantefleurie, that the men called her "Pâquette" – some called her "Pâquerette" (a daisy) – and then she was ruined. We saw directly that she was ruined, one Sunday when she came to church with a gold cross on her neck – At fourteen years of age! think of that! First it was the young Viscount de Cormontreuil, whose castle is about three-quarters of a league from Rheims; then, Messire Henri de Traincourt, the king's equerry; then, something lower, Chiart de Beaulion, sergeant-at-arms; then lower still, Guery Aubergeon, the king's carver; then Macé de Frépus, monsieur the dauphin's barber; then Thévenin le Moine, the king's first cook; then, still descending, to men older and less noble, she fell to Guillaume Racine, viol-player – and to Thierry de Mer, lamp-maker. Then, poor Chantefleurie, she became common property – she was come to the last sou of her gold-piece. What think you, my damoiselles? At the coronation, in the same year '61, it was she that made the bed for the king of the ribalds! – That self-same year! –'

Mahiette sighed, and wiped away a tear that had started to her eyes.

'Here's a story,' said Gervaise, 'that's not very uncommon; and I do not see that it has anything to do with either gypsies or children.'

'Patience!' resumed Mahiette – 'As for a child, we shall soon come to it. In '66, sixteen years ago this month, on Saint Paul's day, Pâquette was brought to bed of a little girl. Poor creature; she was in great joy at it – she had long wished for a child. Her mother, poor simple woman, who'd never known how to do any-thing but shut her eyes; her mother was dead. Pâquette had nothing in the world to love and none to love her. For five years past, since she had gone astray, poor Chantefleurie had been a wretched creature. She was alone, alone in the world; pointed at, shouted after, through the streets; beaten by the sergeants; mocked by little ragged boys. And then she had seen her twentieth year – and twenty is old age for light women. Her wantonness was beginning to bring her in scarcely more than her needlework had formerly. Every fresh wrinkle made a crown less in her pocket; winter became again a hard season; again wood was scarce on her hearth, and bread in her cupboard. She could no longer work; for in giving way to pleasure she had become idle, and she suffered much more than formerly, because when she became idle she longed for pleasure.

'Well, then – she was very sorrowful, very wretched, and her tears wore deep furrows in her cheeks. But in the midst of her shame, her folly and her debauchery, she thought she would be less shameful, less wild and less dissipated, if there were something or some one in the world that she could love, and that could love her. It must be a child, for only a child could be innocent enough for that. She was aware of this after trying to love a thief, the only man that would have anything to say to her – but in a little time she had found out that the thief despised her. Those women of love require either a lover or a child to fill their hearts. Otherwise they are very unhappy. Not being able to find a lover, all her wishes turned toward having a child; and, as she had all along been pious, she prayed to God continually to send her one. So the good God took pity on her and gave her a little girl. I can not describe to you her joy – it was a fury of tears, kisses and caresses. She suckled the child herself; she made it swaddling-clothes out of her coverlet, the only one she had upon her bed; and no longer felt cold or hungry. She became beautiful once more in consequence of it. An old maid makes a young mother. Gallantry claimed her once more; men came again to see La Chantefleurie; she found customers for her wares; and out of all those horrors she made baby-clothes, capes and bibs, lace robes and little satin caps – without so much as thinking of buying herself another coverlet. It is certain that little Agnès – that was the child's name: its Christian name – certain it is that the little thing was more swathed with ribbons and embroideries than a dauphiness of Dauphiny. Among other things, she had a pair of little shoes, the like of which King Louis XI certainly never had. Her mother had stitched and embroidered them herself; she had lavished on them all her skill as an embroideress, and all the embellishments of a robe for the Holy Virgin. They were the two sweetest little pink shoes that ever were seen.

'Pâquette's child had not only pretty feet. I saw her when she was but four months old; she was a little love. Her eyes were larger than her mouth, and she had the most beautiful, fine, dark hair, which already curled. She would have made a superb brunette at sixteen! Her mother became more and more crazy about her every day. She hugged her – kissed her – tickled her – washed her – dressed her out – devoured her!'

'The tale is fair and very good,' said Gervaise, in an undertone, 'but what is there about gypsies in all that?'

'Why, here,' replied Mahiette. 'One day there came to Rheims a very odd sort of gentry. They were beggars and vagabonds, who were roving about the country, headed by their duke and their counts. They were swarthy, their hair all curly, and rings of silver in their ears. The women were still uglier than the men. Their faces were darker, and always uncovered; they wore a sorry kirtle about their body; an old cloth woven with cords, bound upon their shoulder; and their hair hanging like a horse's tail. They came to Rheims to tell fortunes in the name of the King of Algiers and the Emperor of Germany. You can readily imagine that no more was needed for them to be forbidden entrance to the town. Then the whole band encamped of their own accord near the gate of Braine, upon that mound where there's a windmill, close by the old chalk-pits. And all Rheims went to see them. Nevertheless, there were ugly rumors about their child-stealing, purse-cutting and eating of human flesh. The wise folks said to the foolish ones, "Don't go there!" and then went themselves by stealth. It was an infatuation. The fact is, that they said things fit to astonish a cardinal. Mothers boasted loudly of their children after the gypsy-women had read all sorts of miracles in their hands, written in Turkish and Pagan.

'Poor Chantefleurie was seized with curiosity – she had a mind to know what she had got, and whether her pretty little Agnès would not some day be Empress of Armenia, or of elsewhere. So she carried her to the gypsies; and the gypsy-women admired the child, fondled it, kissed it with their black mouths and wondered over its little hand – alas! to the great joy of its mother. They were particularly delighted with the pretty feet and the pretty shoes. The child was not yet a year old. But she was frightened at the gypsy-women, and fell a-crying. Her mother kissed her the harder, and went away overjoyed at the good fortune which the soothsayers had told her Agnès. She was to be beautiful, virtuous and a queen. So she returned to her garret in the Rue Folle Peine, quite proud to carry with her a queen. The next day she took advantage of a moment when the child was asleep on her bed (for she always had it to sleep with herself), gently left the door ajar, and ran to tell a neighbor that the day was to come when her daughter Agnès was to be waited on at the table by the King of England and the Archduke of Ethiopia – and a hundred other marvels. On her return, hearing no sound as she went up the stairs, she said to herself, "Good, the child is still asleep." She found her door wider open than she had left it – the poor mother, however, went in and ran to the bed. The child was no longer there – the place was empty. Nothing remained of the child but one of its pretty shoes. She rushed out of the room, flew down the stairs, and began to beat her head against the wall, crying, "My child! who has my child? who has taken my child?" The street was deserted – the house stood alone – no one could tell her anything about it; she went about the town – searched all the streets – ran hither and thither the whole day, wild, mad, terrible, peeping at the doors and windows like a wild beast that has lost its little ones.

'When night came she went home. During her absence, a neighbor had seen two gypsy-women steal slyly up stairs with a bundle in their arms; then came down again, after shutting the door, and hurry off. After they were gone, something like the cries of a child were heard in Pâquette's room – the mother laughed wildly – ran up the stairs as if on wings – burst in her door like a cannon going off, and entered the room. A frightful thing to tell, Oudarde! – instead of her sweet little Agnès, so fresh and rosy, who was a gift from the good God, there was a sort of little monster, hideous, shapeless, one-eyed, with its limbs all awry, crawling and squalling upon the floor. She hid her eyes in horror. "Oh!" said she, "can it be that the witches have changed my child into that frightful animal!" They carried the little club-footed creature away as quick as possible. He would have driven her mad. He was the monstrous off-spring of some gypsy-woman given over to the devil. He seemed to be about four years old, and spoke a language which was not a human tongue – there were words that were impossible. La Chantefleurie flung herself upon the little shoe, all that was left her of all that she had loved. There she remained so long motionless, speechless, breathless, that they thought she was dead. Suddenly she trembled all over – covered her relic with frantic kisses, and burst out sobbing, as if her heart were broken.

'All at once Chantefleurie sprang up and ran through the streets of Rheims, shouting: "To the gypsies' camp! to the gypsies' camp! Bring guards to burn the witches!" The gypsies were gone – it was pitch dark. No one could follow them. On the morrow, two leagues from Rheims, on a heath between Gueux and Tilloy, the remains of a large fire were found, some ribbons which had belonged to Pâquette's child, drops of blood and some goat's dung. The night just passed happened to be a Saturday night. There could be no further doubt that the Egyptians had held their Witches' Sabbath on that heath, and had devoured the child in company with Beelzebub, as the Mahometans do. When

La Chantefleurie learnt these horrible things, she did not weep – she moved her lips as if to speak, but could not. On the morrow her hair was gray. On the second day she had disappeared.'

' 'Tis in truth a frightful tale!' Oudarde; 'enough to draw tears from a Burgundian!'

'I am no longer surprised,' added Gervaise, 'that the fear of gypsies should haunt you so.'

'And you had all the reason,' resumed Oudarde, 'to flee with your Eustache just now, since these, too, are gypsies.'

Oudarde, a fat and tender-hearted woman, would have been quite content to sigh in company with Mahiette. But Gervaise, more curious, had not yet come to the end of her questions.

'And the monster?' said she all at once to Mahiette.

'What monster?' asked the other.

'The little gypsy monster left by the witches at La Chantefleurie's in exchange for her child. What was done with it? I hope you drowned it, too.'

'Not so,' answered Mahiette.

'What? burned it then? I' faith, that was a better way of disposing of a witch's child.'

'Neither the one nor the other, Gervaise. Monsieur the archbishop took an interest in the child of Egypt; he exorcised it, blessed it, carefully took the devil out of its body, and sent it to Paris to be exposed upon the wooden bed at Notre-dame as a foundling.'

As the three women approached the house of the Tour Roland, Oudarde said to the other two:

'We must not all three look into the hole at once, lest we should frighten the Sachette. You two pretend to read the Dominus in the breviary, while I take a peep at the window-hole. The Sachette knows me a little. I'll tell you when you may come.'

She went to the window alone. The moment that she looked in, profound pity took possession of every feature, and her frank, gay visage altered its expression and color as suddenly as if it had passed from a ray of sunshine to a ray of moonlight. A moment later, she put her finger to her lips and beckoned to Mahiette to come and look.

Mahiette, much moved, joined her silently and on tip-toe, like one approaching a death-bed.

It was in truth a melancholy sight that presented itself to the eyes of the two women, as they gazed through the grated window of the Rat-Hole, neither stirring nor breathing.

The cell was small, broader than it was long, with an arched ceiling, and, seen from within, looked like the inside of a huge bishop's mitre. On the bare flag-stones that formed its floor, in one corner, a woman was sitting, or rather crouching. Her chin rested on her knees, which her crossed arms pressed closely against her breast. Doubled up in this manner, clad in brown sackcloth which covered her loosely from head to foot, her long, gray hair pulled over in front and hanging over her face, down her legs to her feet – she seemed at first only a strange form outlined against the dark background of the cell.

This figure, which looked as if riveted to the flag-stones, seemed to have neither motion, thought, nor breath. In that thin sackcloth, in January, lying on a stone floor, without fire, in the darkness of a dungeon, whose oblique loophole admitted only the chill blast, and never the sun – she appeared not to suffer, not even to feel.

But Mahiette was gazing with an ever increasing anxiety at that wan, withered, disheveled head, and her eyes filled with tears. 'That would indeed be singular!' muttered she.

Passing her head through the bars of the window, she contrived to get a glimpse of the corner upon which the unfortunate woman's eyes were invariably riveted.

When she withdrew her head from the window her cheeks were bathed with tears.

'What do you call that woman?' said she to Oudarde.

Oudarde answered, 'We call her Sister Gudule.'

'And I,' returned Mahiette, 'call her Pâquette la Chantefleurie.'

Then, laying her finger on her lips, she motioned to the amazed Oudarde to put her head through the aperture, and look.

Oudarde looked and saw, in the corner upon which the eye of the recluse was fixed in that gloomy absorption, a tiny shoe of pink satin, embroidered with countless gold and silver spangles.

Eustache noticed that his three conductresses were looking at something through the hole in the wall; and curiosity taking possession of him in turn he climbed upon a stone post, raised himself on tip-toe, and thrusting his red, chubby face through the opening, cried out, 'Mother, let me see, too.'

At the sound of this childish voice, the recluse started. She turned her head with the sharp, abrupt movement of a steel spring; her two long, thin hands brushed back the hair from her forehead; and she fixed upon the child a look of astonishment, bitterness and despair. That look was but a flash.

'Oh, my God!' she exclaimed suddenly, hiding her head upon her knees – and it seemed as if her hoarse voice tore her breast in passing – 'at least do not show me those of others!'

A long shiver ran through her entire frame, from head to foot; her teeth chattered; she half raised her head, pressing her elbows to her sides, and clasping her feet in her hands, as if to warm them.

Her limbs shook, her voice trembled, her eyes flashed. She raised herself upon her knees; suddenly she stretched her thin white hand towards the child, who was looking at her in surprise. 'Take away that child!' she cried, 'the Egyptian woman is about to pass by.'

Then she fell with her face to the ground, and her forehead struck the floor with the sound of one stone upon another. The three women thought her dead. But a moment later she stirred, and they saw her crawl upon her hands and knees to the corner where the little shoe was.

Mahiette, whose utterance had been choked until then, now made an effort. 'Wait,' she said; and then, bending down to the window, 'Pâquette!' she cried, 'Pâquette la Chantefleurie!'

The recluse shook all over; sprang upon her feet, and bounded to the window with eyes flaming that Mahiette and Oudarde and the other woman and the child retreated to the parapet of the quay.

But still the forbidding face of the recluse appeared pressed against the bars of the window. 'Oh, oh!' she cried, with a frightful laugh, ''tis the Egyptian who calls me!'

At this instant the scene which was passing at the pillory caught her wild eye. Her forehead wrinkled with horror – she stretched out of her den her two skeleton arms, and cried out, in a voice that resembled a death-rattle: 'So, 'tis thou once more, daughter of Egypt – 'Tis thou who callest me, stealer of children! Well, be thou accursed! accursed! accursed! – '

4

These words were, so to speak, the connecting link between two scenes which, until that moment, had been simultaneously developing themselves, each upon its particular stage – the one, that which has just been related, at the Trou aux Rats; the other, now to be described, at the pillory. The former was witnessed only by the three women whose acquaintance the reader has just made; the latter had for spectators the whole crowd which we saw some time since collect upon the Place de Grève, around the pillory and the gibbet.

The populace, well accustomed to wait for public executions, did not manifest great impatience. It amused itself looking at the pillory – a very simple sort of structure, consisting of a cubical mass of stonework, some ten feet high, and hollow within. A very steep flight of steps, of unhewn stone, called by distinction the 'ladder', led to the upper platform, upon which was seen a horizontal wheel of solid oak. The victim was bound upon this wheel, on his knees, and his arms pinioned. An upright shaft of timber, set in motion by a capstan concealed inside the little structure, gave a rotary motion to the wheel, which always maintained its horizontal position, thus presenting the face of the culprit successively to each side of the Square in turn. This was called 'turning' a criminal.

At last the culprit arrived, tied to the tail of a cart, and as soon as he was hoisted upon the platform, so that he could be seen from all parts of the Square, bound with cords and straps to the wheel of the pillory, a prodigious hooting, mingled with laughter and acclamations, burst from the assemblage in the Square. They had recognized Quasimodo.

Quasimodo, impassive, did not wince. All resistance on his part was rendered impossible by what was then called, in the language of criminal law, 'the vehemence and firmness of the bonds' – that is to say, that the small straps and chains probably cut into his flesh.

He had allowed himself to be led, thrust, carried, hoisted, bound and bound again. Nothing was to be seen upon his countenance but the astonishment of a savage or an idiot. He was known to be deaf; he seemed to be blind.

They placed him on his knees on the circular plank; he made no resistance. He was stripped of shirt and doublet to the waist; he submitted. They bound him down under a fresh system of straps and buckles; he let them buckle and strap him. Only from time to time he breathed heavily, like a calf, whose head hangs dangling over the side of the butcher's cart.

There was a wild laugh among the crowd when they saw, stripped naked to their view, Quasimodo's hump, his camel breast, his callous and hairy shoulders. Amidst all this mirth, a man of short stature and robust frame, in the livery of the city, ascended the platform, and placed himself by the culprit. His name speedily circulated among the spectators – it was Maître Pierrat Torterue, official torturer at the Châtelet.

He began by depositing on one corner of the pillory a black hour-glass, the upper cup of which was filled with red sand, which was filtering through into the lower receptacle. Then he took off his parti-colored doublet; and there was seen hanging from his right hand a slender whip with long, white thongs, shining, knotted, braided and armed with points of metal. With his left hand he carefully rolled his right shirt-sleeve up to his armpit.

The wheel began to turn; Quasimodo staggered under his bonds. The amazement suddenly depicted upon his deformed visage redoubled the bursts of laughter all around him.

All at once, at the moment when the wheel in its rotation presented to Maître Pierrat Quasimodo's humped back, Maître Pierrat raised his arm, the thin lashes hissed sharply in the air like a handful of vipers, and fell with fury upon the poor wretch's shoulders.

Quasimodo made a spring as if starting from his sleep. He now began to understand. He writhed in his bonds. A violent contraction of surprise and pain distorted the muscles of his face; but he heaved not a sigh. Only he turned his head backward to the right, then to the left, balancing it as a bull does when stung in the flank by a gadfly.

A second stroke followed the first – then a third – then another – and another – and so on and on. The wheel did not cease to turn, nor the blows to rain down.

Soon the blood spurted; it streamed in countless rivulets over the swarthy shoulders of the hunchback; and the slender thongs in their rotary motion which rent the air sprinkled drops of it upon the crowd.

Quasimodo had relapsed, in appearance at least, into his former apathy. At first he had striven, silently and without any great external effort, to burst his bonds. His eye had been seen to kindle, his muscles to stiffen, his limbs to gather all their force and the straps and chains stretched. The effort was powerful, prodigious, desperate – but the old shackles of the provostry resisted. They cracked; and that was all. Quasimodo sank down exhausted. Amazement gave place in his countenance to an expression of bitter and deep discouragement. He closed his only eye, dropped his head upon his breast, and seemed as if he were dead.

Thenceforward he stirred no more. Nothing could wring any motion from him – neither his blood, which continued to flow; nor the blows which fell with redoubled fury; nor the rage of the executioner, who worked himself up and became intoxicated with the execution; nor the noise of the horrid lashes, keener and sharper than the stings of a wasp.

At length an usher of the Châtelet, clothed in black, mounted on a black horse, and stationed by the side of the steps from the commencement of the punishment, extended his ebony wand toward the hour-glass. The executioner stopped. The wheel stopped. Quasimodo's eye slowly reopened.

The flagellation was finished. Two assistants of the official torturer bathed the bleeding shoulders of the sufferer, anointed them with some kind of unguent, which immediately closed all

5   65

the wounds, and threw over his back a sort of yellow cloth cut in the form of a chasuble. Meanwhile Pierrat Torterue let the blood that soaked the lashes of his scourge drain from them in drops upon the ground.

But all was not yet over for Quasimodo. He had still to undergo that hour on the pillory which Maître Florian Barbedienne had so judiciously added to the sentence of Messire Robert d'Estouteville.

The hour-glass was therefore turned, and the hunchback was left bound to the plank, that justice might be fully satisfied.

We have already shown that Quasimodo was generally hated – for more than one good reason, it is true. The joy at seeing him appear thus in the pillory had been universal; and the harsh punishment he had just undergone, and the piteous plight in which it had left him, far from softening the hearts of the populace, had but rendered their hatred more malicious by arming it with the sting of mirth.

Quasimodo was deaf, but his sight was good; and the public fury was not less forcibly expressed on their faces than by their words. Besides, the stones that struck him explained the bursts of laughter.

He bore it for a time. But, by degrees, that patience which had resisted the lash of the torturer relaxed and gave way under these insect stings.

At first he slowly rolled around a look of menace at the crowd. But, shackled as he was, his look was powerless to chase away those flies which galled his wound. He then struggled in his bonds; and his furious contortions made the old wheel of the pillory creak upon its timbers. All which but increased the derision and the hooting.

Then the poor wretch, unable to break the collar which chained him like a wild beast, once more became quiet; only, at intervals, a sigh of rage heaved the hollows of his breast. Moreover, with such a degree of deformity, is infamy a thing that can be felt? But resentment, hatred, despair, slowly spread over that hideous visage a cloud which grew darker and darker, more and more charged with electricity which burst forth in a thousand flashes from the eye of the cyclops.

However, that cloud was lightened for a moment as a mule passed through the crowd, bearing a priest on his back. As far away as he could see that mule and that priest, the poor sufferer's countenance softened. The fury which convulsed it gave way to a strange smile, full of ineffable sweetness, gentleness, tenderness. As the priest approached this smile became more pronounced, more distinct, more radiant. But the moment the mule was near enough to the pillory for its rider to recognize the sufferer, the priest cast down his eyes, wheeled about, clapped spurs to his beast, as if in haste to escape a humiliating appeal, and by no means desirous of being known and addressed by a poor devil in such a situation.

This priest was the Archdeacon Dom Claude Frollo.

Quasimodo's brow was overcast by a darker cloud than ever. The smile was still mingled with it for a time; but bitter, disheartened and profoundly sad.

Time passed. He had been there at least an hour and a half; lacerated, abused, mocked, and almost stoned to death.

All at once he again struggled in his chains, with redoubled desperation, that shook the whole framework that held him; and, breaking the silence which he had hitherto obstinately kept, he cried in a hoarse and furious voice, which was more like a bark than a human cry, and which drowned the noise of the hooting, 'Water!'

This exclamation of distress, far from exciting compassion, heightened the mirth of the good people of Paris who surrounded the pillory. Not a voice was raised around the unhappy victim, except to jeer at his thirst. Certainly he was at this moment more grotesque and repulsive than he was pitiable – with his face purple and dripping, his wild eye, his mouth foaming with rage and suffering, and his tongue lolling half out.

In a few minutes, Quasimodo cast a despairing look upon the crowd, and repeated in a still more heart-rending voice, 'Water!'

Everyone laughed.

At that moment, he saw the populace make way. A young girl, fantastically dressed, emerged from the throng. She was followed by a little white goat with gilded horns, and carried a tambourine in her hand.

Quasimodo's eye sparkled. It was the gypsy-girl whom he had attempted to carry off the night before, for which piece of presumption he had some confused notion that they were punishing him at that very moment – which, in point of fact, was not in the least the case, since he was punished only for the misfortune of being deaf and of being tried by a deaf judge. He doubted not that she, too, was come to take her revenge, and to deal her blow like all the rest.

Thus, he beheld her rapidly ascend the steps. He was choking with rage and vexation. He would have liked to crumble the pillory to atoms; and could the flash of his eye have dealt death, the gypsy would have been reduced to ashes before she could have reached the platform.

Without a word, she approached the sufferer, who writhed in a vain effort to escape her; and detaching a gourd from her girdle, she raised it gently to the poor wretch's parched lips.

Then in that eye, hitherto so dry and burning, a big tear was seen to start, which fell slowly down that misshapen face so long convulsed by despair. It was possibly the first that the unfortunate creature had ever shed.

Meanwhile, he forgot to drink. The gypsy-girl made her little pout with impatience; and smiling, pressed the neck of the gourd to the tusked mouth of Quasimodo.

He drank deep draughts. His thirst was burning.

When he had done, the poor wretch put out his black lips, undoubtedly to kiss the fair hand which had just succored him; but the young girl, who, remembering the violent attempt of the preceding night, was perhaps not without some mistrust, drew back her hand with the frightful gesture of a child afraid of being bitten by some animal.

Then the poor deaf creature fixed upon her a look of reproach and unutterable sorrow.

It would have been a touching sight anywhere – this beautiful, fresh, pure, charming girl, who was at the same time so weak, thus piously hastening to the relief of so much wretchedness, deformity and malevolence. On a pillory the spectacle was sublime.

The very populace were moved by it, and clapped their hands, shouting, 'Noël, Noël!'

It was at that moment that the recluse caught sight from the loophole of her cell of the gypsy-girl on the pillory, and hurled at her her sinister imprecation, 'Accursed be thou, daughter of Egypt! accursed! accursed!'

BOOK FIVE

1

Several weeks had passed.

It was now the beginning of March. It was one of those days of the early spring which are so mild and beautiful that all Paris turns out into the squares and promenades, and celebrates them as if they were Sundays. On days so brilliant, so warm, and so serene, there is one hour in particular, at which one should go and admire the portal of Notre-Dame.

It was just that hour.

Opposite the lofty cathedral, reddened by the setting sun, upon a stone balcony, over the porch of a handsome Gothic house, at the corner of the Place and the Rue du Parvis, some lovely young girls were laughing and chatting gracefully and playfully.

It was easy to divine that they were noble and wealthy heirresses. They were, in fact, all damsels of good birth, assembled at that moment at the house of the widowed lady of De Gondelaurier. The damsels in question had been entrusted by their parents to the care of the discreet and venerable Madame Aloïse de Gondelaurier, widow of a former master of the king's crossbowmen, now living in retirement with their only daughter, at her house in the Place do Parvis-Notre-Dame, at Paris.

The balcony on which these young girls were opened into an apartment richly hung with fawn-colored Flanders leather stamped with golden foliage. At the farther end, by a high fireplace, covered with armorial bearings and escutcheons from top to bottom, sat in a rich crimson velvet armchair, the lady of Gondelaurier, whose fifty-five years were as plainly written in her dress as on her face.

By her side stood a young man of imposing though somewhat vain and swaggering mien, one of those handsome fellows about whom all women agree, though the grave and discerning men shake their heads at them. This young cavalier wore the brilliant uniform of a captain of the archers of the household troops.

From time to time, the old lady addressed him in a low voice, and he replied as best he could, with awkward and forced courtesy. From the smiles and significant gestures of Madame Aloïse, from the glances she threw toward her daughter Fleur-de-Lys as

69

she spoke low to the captain, it was evident that there was here a question of some betrothal concluded, some marriage near at hand, no doubt, between the young man and Fleur-de-Lys. And from the cold embarrassed air of the officer, it was easy to see that on his side at least there was no question of love. His whole manner expressed constraint and weariness, which a modern French subaltern on garrison duty would admirably render by the exclamation, 'What a beastly bore!'

The good lady, infatuated, as any silly mother might be, with her daughter's charms, did not perceive the officer's want of enthusiasm, but exerted herself in a low voice to attract his attention to the infinite grace with which Fleur-de-Lys plied her needle or wound a skein of silk.

'Speak to her,' said Madame Aloïse, pushing him by the shoulder; 'say something to her; you're grown quite timid.'

We can assure the reader that timidity was neither a virtue nor a defect of the captain. He endeavored, however, to do as he was bid.

'Fair cousin,' said he, approaching Fleur-de-Lys, 'what is the subject of this tapestry which keeps you so busy?'

'Gentle cousin,' answered Fleur-de-Lys, in a pettish tone, 'I have already told you three times; it is the grotto of Neptunus.'

It was evident that Fleur-de-Lys saw more clearly than her mother through the cold, absent manner of the captain. He felt that he must needs make conversation.

'And for whom is all this fine Neptune-work intended?' asked he.

'For the abbey of Saint-Antoine des Champs,' said Fleur-de-Lys, without raising her eyes.

There was still an offended tone perceptible in the few words uttered by Fleur-de-Lys. The young man understood that it was indispensable he should whisper in her ear some pretty nothing, some gallant compliment – no matter what. He accordingly leaned over, but his imagination could furnish nothing more tender or familiar than this: 'Why does your mother always wear that petticoat embroidered with her arms, like our grandmothers of Charles VII's time? Pray tell her, fair cousin, that it's not the fashion of the present day.'

Fleur-de-Lys raised her fine eyes toward his reproachfully:

'Is that all you have to say to me?' said she in a low tone.

The captain, more and more embarrassed, returned to the subject of the tapestry. 'It is really a beautiful piece of work!' he cried.

At this moment, Bérangère de Champchevrier, a little sylph of seven years of age, who was gazing into the square through the trefoils of the balcony railing, cried out, 'Oh! do look, dear god-

70

mamma Fleur-de-Lys, at that pretty dancing-girl who is dancing on the pavement, and playing the tambourine among the people yonder!'

'Let us see! Let us see!' cried her lively companions, running to the front of the balcony, while Fleur-de-Lys, musing over the coldness of her affianced lover, followed slowly; and the latter, released by this incident, which cut short an embarrassing conversation, returned to the farther end of the room with the satisfied air of a soldier relieved from duty. And yet no unpleasing service was that of the lovely Fleur-de-Lys; and such it had once appeared to him; but the captain had by degrees become weary of it, and the prospect of an approaching marriage grew less attractive to him each day. Besides, he was of a fickle disposition; and, if the truth must be told, rather vulgar in his tastes. He delighted in the tavern and its accompaniments, and was never at his ease save amidst coarse witticisms, military gallantries, easy beauties, and as easy conquests. He had notwithstanding received from his family some education and polish.

Though still continuing to visit her occasionally, prompted by some small remnant of common respect, he felt doubly constrained with Fleur-de-Lys. In the first place, because he distributed his love so promiscuously that he had but little left for her; and in the second, because, surrounded by a number of stately, starched and modest ladies, he was constantly in fear lest his tongue, accustomed to the language of oaths, should inadvertently break through its bounds and let slip some unfortunate tavern-slang.

He had been for some minutes thinking, or not thinking, but leaning in silence against the carved mantelpiece, when Fleur-de-Lys turning suddenly, addressed him – for after all, the poor girl only pouted in self-defence:

'Gentle cousin, did you not tell us of a little gypsy-girl you saved from a parcel of thieves a month or more ago, as you were on the night patrol?'

'I believe I did, fair cousin,' said the captain.

'Well,' rejoined she, 'perhaps it is that very gypsy-girl who is now dancing in the Parvis. Come and see if you recognize her, cousin Phœbus.'

Phœbus looked, and said:

'Yes – I know her by her goat.'

'Godmamma,' exclaimed Bérangère, whose eyes, incessantly in motion, were suddenly raised toward the top of the towers of Notre-Dame, 'who is that black man up there?'

All the girls raised their eyes. A man was indeed leaning with his elbows upon the topmost balustrade of the northern tower, overlooking the Grève. It was the figure of a priest; and they

71

could clearly discern both his costume and his face resting on both his hands. He was motionless as a statue. His steady gaze was riveted on the Place.

'It is monsieur the Archdeacon of Josas,' said Fleur-de-Lys. 'Fair cousin Phœbus since you know this little gypsy-girl beckon to her to come up. It will amuse us.'

'Why! 'tis not worth while,' replied Phœbus. 'She has no doubt forgotten me; and I know not even her name. However, since you wish it, ladies, I will try.' And leaning over the balustrade of the balcony, he began to call out – 'Little one!'

The dancing-girl was not at that moment playing her tambourine. She turned her head toward the point whence this call proceeded; her brilliant eyes rested on Phœbus, and she stopped short suddenly.

'Little one,' repeated the captain, and he beckoned to her to come in.

The young girl looked at him again; then blushed as if a flame had risen to her cheeks; and, taking her tambourine under her arm, she made her way through the midst of the gaping spectators, toward the door of the house where Phœbus was, with slow, faltering steps, and with the agitated look of a bird yielding to the fascination of a serpent.

A moment or two after, the tapestry door hanging was raised, and the gypsy appeared on the threshold of the room, blushing, confused, breathless, her large eyes cast down, and not daring to advance a step farther.

The captain was the first to break silence.

'Upon my word,' said he, with his tone of brainless assurance, 'here is a charming creature! What think you of her, fair cousin?'

This remark, which a more delicate admirer would at least have made in an undertone, did not tend to dissipate the feminine jealousies which were on the alert in the presence of the gypsy-girl.

Fleur-de-Lys answered the captain with a simpering affectation of disdain – 'Not bad.'

The others whispered together.

'My pretty girl,' said Phœbus, with emphasis, taking several steps towards her, 'I do not know whether I have the supreme felicity of being recognized by you.'

She interrupted him with a look and smile of infinite sweetness.

'Oh! yes,' said she.

'Well, now,' resumed Phœbus, 'you escaped nimbly the other evening. Did I frighten you?'

'Oh! no,' said the gypsy.

There was, in the intonation of that 'Oh! no', uttered after that 'Oh! yes', an ineffable something which wounded Fleur-de-Lys.

'You left me in your stead, my beauty,' continued the captain, whose tongue became unloosed while speaking to a girl from the streets, 'a rare grim-faced fellow, hump-backed and one-eyed, the ringer of the bishop's bells, I believe. They tell me he's an arch-deacon's bastard and a devil by birth. What the deuce could that screech-owl want with you? Hey, tell me!'

'I do not know,' she replied.

'What insolence! But he paid pretty dear for it. Maître Pierrat Torterue is as rough a groom as ever curried a rascal; and your ringer's hide — if that will please you — got a thorough dressing at his hands, I warrant you.'

'Poor man!' said the gypsy-girl — the scene of the pillory brought back to her remembrance by these words.

The captain burst out laughing. 'By the bull's horns! here's pity about as well placed as a feather in a pig's tail. May I have a belly like a pope, if . . .'

He stopped suddenly short. 'Pardon me, ladies — I fear I was about to let slip some nonsense or other.'

'He speaks to this creature in her own language,' added Fleur-de-Lys in an undertone, her irritation increasing every moment. This irritation was not diminished by seeing the captain, delighted with the gypsy, and most of all with himself, turn round on his heel and repeat with coarse, naïve and soldier-like gallantry: 'A lovely girl, upon my soul!'

'Very barbarously dressed!' said Diane de Christeuil, with the smile which showed her fine teeth.

The gypsy-girl was not insensible to this pin-prick. A glow of shame, or a flash of anger inflamed her eyes or her cheeks, but she remained motionless; she fixed on Phœbus a sad, sweet, resigned look. There was also happiness and tenderness in that gaze. It seemed as if she restrained herself for fear of being driven away.

Phœbus laughed and took the gypsy's part, with a mixture of pity and impertinence.

'Let them talk, little one,' repeated he, jingling his gold spurs; 'doubtless, your dress is a little wild and extravagant; but in a charming girl like you, what does that signify?'

'Dear me!' exclaimed the blonde Gaillefontaine, drawing up her swan-like throat with a bitter smile, 'I see that messieurs the king's archers take fire easily at bright gypsy eyes.'

'And why not?' said Phœbus.

The gypsy, who had dropped her eyes on the floor as Gaillefontaine spoke, raised them beaming with joy and pride, and fixed them once more on Phœbus. She was very beautiful at that moment.

The old dame, who was watching this scene, felt offended without understanding why.

'Holy Virgin!' cried she suddenly, 'what's that about my leg? Ah! the villainous beast!'

It was the goat which had just arrived in search of its mistress, and which, in hurrying toward her, had entangled its horns in the load of drapery which the noble dame's garments heaped around her when she was seated.

The gypsy crouched upon her knees, and pressed her cheek against the caressing head of the goat. It seemed as if she were asking its pardon for having left it behind.

At that moment Fleur-de-Lys noticed a little bag of embroidered leather hung round the goat's neck.

'What is that?' she asked of the gypsy.

The girl raised her large eyes toward her, and replied gravely, 'That is my secret.'

'I should like to know your secret,' thought Fleur-de-Lys.

Meanwhile, the good dame had risen angrily. 'Come, come, gypsy, if neither you nor your goat have anything to dance to us, what are you doing here?'

The gypsy directed her steps slowly toward the door without making any reply. But the nearer she approached it, the slower were her steps. An irresistible magnet seemed to retard her. Suddenly, she turned, her eyes moistened with tears toward Phœbus, and stood still.

'Zounds!' cried the captain, 'you shall not go away thus. Come back and dance for us something. By-the-by, my beauty, what's your name?'

'Esmeralda,' said the dancer, without taking her eyes off him.

Meanwhile, Bérangère, without attracting attention, had, a few minutes before, enticed the goat into a corner of the room with a piece of nut-cake. In an instant they had become good friends; and the curious child had untied the little bag which hung at the goat's neck, had opened it, and spread the contents on the matting; it was an alphabet, each letter being inscribed separately on a small tablet of wood. No sooner were the toys displayed upon the matting, than the child saw, with surprise, the goat (one of whose miracles, doubtless, it was) select with her gilded hoof certain letters, and arrange them in a particular order by gently pushing them together. In a moment they formed a word which the goat seemed practised in composing, so slight was her hesitation; and Bérangère suddenly cried out, clasping her hands with admiration:

'Godmamma Fleur-de-Lys – do see what the goat has been doing!'

Fleur-de-Lys hastened to look, and suddenly started. The letters arranged on the floor formed this word,

PHOEBUS

'Here's the secret!' thought Fleur-de-Lys.

Meanwhile, at the child's exclamation they had all hurried forward to look; the mother, the young ladies, the gypsy, and the officer.

The gypsy saw the blunder the goat had committed. She turned red – then pale – and began to tremble like a culprit before the captain, who regarded her with a smile of satisfaction and astonishment.

'*Phoebus!*' whispered the girls, in amazement, 'that's the captain's name!'

'You have a wonderful memory!' said Fleur-de-Lys to the stupefied gypsy. Then bursting into sobs: 'Oh,' stammered she tearfully, hiding her face between her two fair hands, 'she is a sorceress!' while she heard a voice yet more bitter whisper from her inmost heart, 'she is a rival!'

She fell fainting to the floor.

'My child! my child!' cried the terrified mother. 'Begone, you fiendish gypsy!'

Esmeralda gathered together the unlucky letters in the twinkling of an eye, made a sign to Djali, and quitted the room at one door as Fleur-de-Lys was being carried out through the other.

Captain Phoebus, left alone, hesitated a moment between the two doors; then followed the gypsy.

2

The priest whom the young ladies had observed on the top of the northern tower, leaning over toward the Square, and so attentive to the gypsy-girl's dancing, was, in fact, the Archdeacon Claude Frollo.

Every day, an hour before sunset, the archdeacon ascended the staircase of the tower and shut himself up in his cell, where he sometimes passed whole nights. On this day, just as he had reached the low door of his retreat, the sound of a tambourine and castanets reached his ear. This sound proceeded from the Square in front of the cathedral. The cell, as we have already said, had but one window, looking upon the back of the church. Claude Frollo had hastily withdrawn the key, and in an instant was on the summit of the tower, in that gloomy, thoughtful attitude in which the young ladies had first seen him.

It would have been difficult to say what was the nature of that glance, or whence arose the flame that issued from it. It was a fixed gaze, but full of tumult and perturbation. And yet from the profound quiescence of his whole body, scarcely shaken now and then by an involuntary shiver, from the rigidity of his arms, more marble-like than the balustrade on which they leaned; from the petrified smile which contracted his countenance, one might have said that no part of Claude Frollo was alive but his eyes.

The gypsy-girl was dancing, twirling her tambourine on the tip of her finger, and tossing it in the air as she danced Provençal sarabands; agile, light, joyous and unconscious of the formidable gaze which fell directly on her head.

The crowd swarmed around her; from time to time, a man, tricked out in a red and yellow coat, went round to make them keep the ring; then returned, seated himself in a chair a few paces from the dancer, and took the goat's head on his knees. This man appeared to be the companion of the gypsy. Claude Frollo, from his elevated post, could not distinguish his features.

From the moment that the archdeacon perceived this stranger his attention seemed divided between the dancer and him, and his countenance became more and more sombre. All at once he started up, and a thrill shook his whole frame. 'Who can that man be?' he muttered between his teeth. 'Until now I have always seen her alone.'

He then plunged down under the winding vault of the spiral staircase, and once more descended. In passing the door of the belfry, which was ajar, he saw something which struck him; he beheld Quasimodo, who, leaning out of one of the apertures in those great slate eaves which resemble enormous blinds, was likewise gazing into the Square. He was so absorbed in profound contemplation that he was not aware of his adoptive father passing by. His wild eye had a singular expression; it was a charmed, tender look. 'Strange!' murmured Claude; 'can it be the Egyptian at whom he is thus looking?' He continued his descent. In a few minutes the moody archdeacon sallied forth into the Square by the door at the base of the tower.

'What has become of the gypsy?' said he, mingling with the group of spectators which the sound of the tambourine had collected.

'I know not,' answered one of those nearest him; 'she has but just disappeared. I think she is gone to dance some of her fan-

76

dangos in the house opposite, whither they called her.'

In the place of the gypsy-girl, upon the same carpet whose arabesques but a moment before had seemed to vanish beneath the fantastic figures of her dance, the archdeacon saw no one but the red and yellow man, who, in order to earn a few testers in his turn, was parading around the circle, his elbows in his hips, his head thrown back, his face red, his neck out-stretched, with a chair between his teeth. On this chair he had tied a cat, which a woman of the neighborhood had lent him, and which was spitting in great affright.

'By Our Lady!' cried the archdeacon, just as the mountebank, perspiring heavily, passed in front of him with his pyramid of chair and cat; 'what does Maître Pierre Gringoire there?'

The harsh voice of the archdeacon threw the poor devil into such commotion that he lost his equilibrium, and down fell the whole edifice, chair and cat and all, pell-mell upon the heads of the bystanders in the midst of inextinguishable hootings.

It is probable that Maître Pierre Gringoire (for he indeed it was) would have had a sorry account to settle with the neighbor who owned the cat, and all the bruised and scratched faces around him, if he had not hastened to profit by the tumult to take refuge in the church, whither Claude Frollo had motioned to him to follow.

The cathedral was already dark and deserted; the transepts were full of shadows, and the lamps of the chapels twinkled like stars, so black had the arched roofs become. Only the great rose-window of the façade, whose thousand tints were steeped in a ray of horizontal sunlight, glistened in the dark like a cluster of diamonds, and threw its dazzling reflection to the other end of the nave.

When they had proceeded a few steps, Dom Claude leaned his back against a pillar and looked steadfastly at Gringoire. There was nothing mocking or ironical in the priest's glance; it was serious, calm and searching. The archdeacon was the first to break silence.

'Come, now, Maître Pierre,' said he, 'you are to explain many things to me. And first of all, how comes it that you have not been seen these two months, and that now one finds you in the public squares, in rare guise, i' faith, half red, half yellow?'

'Messire,' said Gringoire, piteously, 'it is in sooth a monstrous garb, and behold me about as comfortable in it as a cat with a calabash clapped on her head. But what could I do, reverend master? 'Tis the fault of my ancient jerkin, which basely forsook me at the beginning of the winter, under the pretext that it was falling into tatters, and that it required repose in the basket of a rag-picker. What was to be done? This garment offered itself —

I took it, and left off my old black frock, which, for a hermetic like myself, was far from being hermetically closed. Behold me, then, in my buffoon's habit, like Saint Genest. What would you have?'

Dom Claude listened in silence. All at once his hollow eyes assumed an expression so sagacious and penetrating that Gringoire felt himself, so to speak, searched to the bottom of the soul by that look.

'Very good, Maître Pierre; but how comes it that you are now in company with that gypsy-dancer?'

'I'faith,' said Gringoire, ''tis because she is my wife and I am her husband.'

The dark eye of the priest flashed fire.

'And hast thou done that, miserable man?' he cried, seizing Gringoire's arm with fury; 'and hast thou been so abandoned by God as to lay thy hand upon that girl?'

'By my hope of Paradise, monseigneur,' answered Gringoire, trembling in every limb, 'I swear to you that I have never touched her – if that be what disturbs you.'

'But what speakest thou, then, of husband and wife?' said the priest.

Gringoire eagerly related to him, as succinctly as possible, what the reader already knows – his adventure of the Cour des Miracles, and his marriage by the broken jug. It appeared, moreover, that this marriage had led to no results whatever, and that each evening the gypsy-girl contrived to cheat him of his nuptials, as she had done on the first night. ''Tis a mortification,' he said in conclusion; 'but that comes of my having had the misfortune to wed a virgin.'

'What mean you?' asked the archdeacon, whose agitation had gradually subsided.

''Tis a superstition. My wife is, according to what an old thief, who is called among us the Duke of Egypt, has told me, a foundling. She wears on her neck an amulet, which it is affirmed will some day cause her to find her parents again, but which would lose its virtue if the young maid were to lose hers. Hence it follows that both of us remain quite virtuous.'

'So,' resumed Claude, whose brow cleared more and more, 'you believe, Maître Pierre, that this creature has not been approached by any man?'

'What chance, Dom Claude, can a man have against a super-stition? She has got that into her head. I assuredly esteem as a rarity this nun-like prudery which is preserved untamed amid those gypsy-girls who are so easily brought into subjection.'

The archdeacon pressed Gringoire with questions.

La Esmeralda was, in Gringoire's opinion, an inoffensive,

charming, pretty creature, with the exception of the pout peculiar to herself – an artless and warm-hearted girl, ignorant of everything, and enthusiastic about everything, not yet aware of the difference between a man and a woman, even in her dreams; just simple like that; fond, above all things, of dancing, of bustle, of the open air. In all the town, she believed herself to be hated by two persons only, of whom she often spoke with dread: the Sachette of the Tour-Roland, a miserable recluse, who bore a secret grudge against gypsy-women, and who cursed the poor dancing-girl every time she passed before her loophole; and a priest who never met her without casting upon her looks and words that affrighted her. The mention of this latter circumstance disturbed the archdeacon greatly, though Gringoire scarcely noticed his perturbation; the two months that had elapsed having been quite sufficient to make the heedless poet forget the singular details of that night when he had first met with the gypsy-girl, and the presence of the archdeacon on that occasion. Otherwise the little dancer feared nothing. She did not tell fortunes, and so was secure from those prosecutions for magic that were so frequently instituted against the gypsy-women. And then, Gringoire was as a brother to her, if not as a husband. After all, the philosopher very patiently endured this kind of Platonic marriage. At any rate he was sure of food and lodging. Every evening he returned with her under the same roof, let her bolt herself in her own little chamber, and slept the sleep of the just – a very agreeable existence on the whole, said he, and very favorable to reverie. And then, in his heart and conscience, the philosopher was not very sure that he was madly in love with the gypsy. He loved her goat almost as much. It was a charming, gentle, intelligent, clever animal; a learned goat. However, the witchcraft of the goat with the gilded hoofs were very harmless tricks indeed. Gringoire explained them to the archdeacon, whom these particulars seemed to interest deeply. In most cases it was sufficient to present the tambourine to the goat in such or such a manner, in order to obtain from it the trick desired. It had been trained to that by the gypsy, who possessed, in these delicate arts, so rare a talent that two month had sufficed to teach the goat to write with moveable letters the word 'Phœbus.'

'Phœbus!' said the priest. 'Why Phœbus?'

'I know not,' replied Gringoire; 'perhaps it is a word which she believes endowed with some magical and secret virtue. She often repeats it in an undertone when she thinks she is alone.'

'Are you sure,' rejoined Claude, with his penetrating look, 'that it is only a word and not a name?'

'Name of whom?' said the poet.

79

'How should I know?' said the priest.

The archdeacon dropped his chin into his hand and appeared to reflect for a moment. Then suddenly turning to Gringoire:

'And thou wilt swear that thou has never touched her?'

'Who?' said Gringoire. 'The goat?'

'No – that woman.'

'My wife? I swear to you I have not.'

'Swear to me by thy mother's womb,' repeated the archdeacon violently, 'that thou has not so much as touched that creature with the tip of thy finger.'

'I could also swear it by my father's head, for the two things have more than one affinity. But, my reverend master, permit me a question in my turn.'

'Speak, sir.'

'What concern is it of yours?'

The pale face of the archdeacon crimsoned like the cheek of a girl. He kept silence for a moment, then answered with visible embarrassment:

'Hearken, Maître Pierre Gringoire. You are not yet damned, so far as I know. I take an interest in you, and wish you well. Now, the least contact with this Egyptian child of the devil would make you a vassal of Satan. 'Tis the body, you know, which ruins the soul. Woe to you, if you approach that woman. That is all.'

'I tried once,' said Gringoire, scratching his ear; 'it was the first day, but I got stung.'

'You had that effrontery, Maître Pierre?'

And the priest's brow darkened again.

'Another time,' continued the poet, smiling, 'before I went to bed, I peeped through the keyhole, and I behold the most delicious damsel in her shift that ever made a bed creak under her bare foot.'

'Get thee gone to the devil!' cried the priest, with a terrible look; and pushing the amazed Gringoire by the shoulders, he plunged with long strides beneath the darkest arches of the cathedral.

Since his morning on the pillory, the inhabitants in the neighborhood of Norte-Dame thought they noticed that Quasimodo's bell-ringing ardor had grown cool. Formerly the bells were going on all occasions. The old church, vibrating and sonorous, was in a perpetual joyous whirl of bells. Some spirit of noise and caprice seemed to sing continuously through those mouths of brass. Now that spirit seemed to have departed. Quasimodo, nevertheless, was still there; what had happened to him, then? was it that the shame and despair of the pillory still rankled in his heart, that the lashes of his tormentor's whip reverberated unceasingly in his soul, and that his grief at such treatment had wholly extinguished in him even his passion for the bells? Or was it rather that Marie had a rival in the heart of the ringer of Notre-Dame, and that the big bell and her fourteen sisters were neglected for something more beautiful and pleasing?

It happened that in the year of Our Lord 1482, the Annunciation fell on Tuesday, the 25th of March. On that day the air was so pure and light that Quasimodo felt some returning affection for his bells.

Having reached the high loft of the belfry, Quasimodo gazed for some time, with a sorrowful shake of the head, on his six songstresses, as if lamenting that some other object had intruded into his heart between them and him. But when he had set them in motion — when he felt that cluster of bells moving under his hand — when he saw, for he did not hear it, the palpitating octave ascend and descend that sonorous scale like a bird hopping from branch to branch; he forgot everything, and his heart expanding made his countenance radiant.

All at once, letting his glance fall between the large slate scales which covered, at a certain height, the perpendicular wall of the belfry, he descried on the Square a young girl fantastically dressed, who stopped, spread out on the ground a carpet on which a little goat came and placed itself, and around whom a group of spectators made a circle. This view suddenly changed the course of his ideas, and congealed his musical enthusiasm as a breath of air congeals melted rosin. He stopped, turned his back to the bells, and crouched behind the slate eaves, fixing on the dancer that thoughtful, tender and softened look which had already astonished the archdeacon on one occasion. Meanwhile, the forgotten bells died away abruptly and all together, to the great disappointment of the lovers of chimes who were listening to the peal.

4

It chanced that upon one fine morning in this same month of March our young college friend, Jehan Frollo du Moulin, perceived, as he was dressing himself, that his breeches, which contained his purse, emitted no metallic sound. 'Poor purse!' said he, drawing it forth from his pocket. 'What! not one little parisis! How cruelly have dice, beer-pots and Venus depleted thee! Behold thee empty, wrinkled and limp!'

He dressed himself sadly. A thought struck him as he was lacing his boots, but he at first rejected it; nevertheless, it returned, and he put on his waistcoat wrong side out, an evident sign of a violent internal struggle. At last he dashed his cap vehemently on the ground, and exclaimed: 'Be it so! come what may, I'll go to my brother. I shall catch a sermon, but I shall also catch a crown.'

He then hastily donned his fur-trimmed jacket, picked up his cap, and rushed out like a madman.

Crossing the Petit-Pont, and striding down the Rue Neuve-Sainte-Geneviève, Jehan de Molendino found himself in front of Notre-Dame. Then all his indecision returned, and he walked about for some moments around the statue of M. Le Gris, repeating to himself with anguish, 'The sermon is sure, the crown piece is doubtful.'

He stopped a beadle who was coming from the cloisters – 'Where is monsieur the Archdeacon of Josas?'

'I believe he is in his cell in the tower,' said the beadle; 'and I would not advise you to disturb him there unless you come from someone like the pope or the king himself.'

Jehan clapped his hands.

'By Satan! here is a splendid opportunity for seeing the famous sorcery-box!'

Being brought to a decision by this reflection, he boldly entered through the little, dark doorway, and began to ascend the winding staircase of Saint Gilles, which leads to the upper stories of the tower.

Reaching the gallery of little columns, he stopped to breathe a moment, swearing against the interminable staircase by we know not how many million cart-loads of devils; he then continued his ascent by the narrow door of the northern tower, which is now closed to the public. Just after he had passed the cage of the bells, he came upon a little landing-place, built in a lateral recess, and, under the arch, a low pointed door; while a loophole opposite, in the circular wall of the staircase, enabled him to discern its enormous lock and strong iron bars.

'Whew!' said the scholar, ' 'Tis here, no doubt.'

The key was in the lock. The door was closed to him; he pushed it gently, and put his head through the opening.

It was a gloomy, dimly-lighted retreat. There was a large armchair and a large table; compasses; alembics; skeletons of animals suspended from the ceiling; a globe rolling on the floor; hippocephali pell-mell with glass jars in which quivered leaf gold; skulls placed on parchments scrawled over with figures and letters; thick manuscripts piled up, all open, without any pity for the cracking corners of the parchment; in short, all the rubbish of science; dust and cobwebs covering the whole heap.

And yet the cell was not deserted. A man sat in the armchair, bending over the table. Jehan, to whom his back was turned, could only see his shoulders and the back of his head; but he had no difficulty in recognizing that bald head, which Nature had provided with an everlasting tonsure, as if wishing to mark, by this outward symbol, the archdeacon's irresistible clerical vocation.

Jehan accordingly recognized his brother; but the door had been opened so gently that Dom Claude was not aware of his presence. The inquisitive student availed himself of the opportunity to examine the cell for a few moments at his leisure. A large furnace, which he had not at first observed, was to the left of the armchair, beneath the dormer-window. On the furnace were heaped in disorder all sorts of vessels – earthenware flasks, glass retorts, coal mattresses. Jehan noticed with a sigh that there was not a single saucepan. 'The kitchen utensils are cold!' thought he.

In fact, there was no fire in the furnace, nor did it appear to have been lighted for a considerable time.

The general appearance of the cell, in short, was one of neglect and ruin; and the sorry condition of the utensils led to the conjecture that their owner had for some time been distracted from his labors by other cares.

Seeing that the archdeacon remained immobile, Jehan withdrew his head very softly, and made some noise with his feet outside the door, like someone just arriving and giving notice of his approach.

'Come in,' cried the archdeacon from the interior of his cell.

'I was expecting you; I left the key in the door purposely; come in, Maître Jacques.'

The student entered boldly. The archdeacon, much annoyed by such a visit in such a place, started in his chair. 'What! is it you, Jehan?'

''Tis a J, at any rate,' said the student, with his ruddy, merry and impudent face.

The countenance of Dom Claude resumed its usual, severe expression.

'What brings you hither?'

'Brother,' replied the student, endeavoring to assume a decent, serious and modest demeanor, twirling his cap in his hands with an air of innocence, 'I am come to ask of you –'

'What?'

'A little moral lecture, of which I have great need.'

'Sir,' said the archdeacon in a cold tone, 'I am greatly displeased with you.'

'Alas!' sighed the student.

'What do you want?' said he, dryly.

'Well, in point of fact, this,' answered Jehan, bravely, 'I need money.'

'And what would you do with it?'

This question caused a flash of hope to gleam before Jehan's eyes. He resumed his demure, caressing manner.

'Hark you, dear brother Claude – I would not come to you with any evil intention. It is not to cut a dash in the taverns with your money, or to parade the streets of Paris in gold brocade trappings, with my lackeys – *cum meo laquasio*. No, brother; 'tis for a good work.'

'What good work?' asked Claude, somewhat surprised.

'Two of my friends wish to purchase an outfit for the infant of a poor Haudriette widow – it is a charity – it will cost three florins, and I should like to contribute my share.'

'And,' continued the shrewd Claude, 'what sort of an infant's outfit is it that is to cost three florins and that for the child of a Haudriette? Since when have the Haudriette widows taken to having brats in swaddling-clothes?'

Jehan broke the ice once more. 'Well, then, I want some money to go and see Isabeau la Thierrye, tonight, at the Val d'Amour.'

'Impure wretch!' exclaimed the priest.

'Only one poor little penny, brother,' persisted the supplicant Jehan. 'I'll learn Gratian by heart – I'll believe well in God – I'll be a perfect Pythagoras of science and virtue! Only one little penny, for pity's sake! Would you have me devoured by famine, whose jaws are gaping before me, blacker, deeper and more noisome than Tartarus or than a monk's nose?'

Dom Claude shook his wrinkled head.

'Well, then,' cried he, 'to the devil! Now for a joyous time! I'll go to the tavern – I'll fight – I'll break pots, and go and see the wenches!'

Thereupon he hurled his cap at the wall, and snapped his fingers like castanets.

The archdeacon eyed him with gloomy look.

'Jehan, you are on a very slippery, downward path; know you whither you are going?'

'To the tavern,' said Jehan.

'Jehan, Jehan! The end will be bad.'

' 'Twill have had a good beginning.'

At this moment the sound of a footfall was heard on the stair.

'Silence!' said the archdeacon, putting his finger to his lip, 'here is Maître Jacques. Hark you, Jehan,' added he, in a low tone, 'beware of ever speaking of what you have seen and heard here. Hide yourself quickly under this furnace, and do not breathe.'

The student crept under the furnace, and there a happy thought struck him.

'By the way, brother Claude – a florin for not breathing!'

'Silence! I promise it.'

'You must give it to me.'

'Take it, then!' said the archdeacon, throwing him his pouch angrily. Jehan crept under the furnace again, and the door opened.

5

The personage who entered wore a black gown and a gloomy mien. He was very gray and wrinkled, bordering on sixty; his eyes blinked, his eyebrows were white, his lip pendulous and his hands large.

The archdeacon, meanwhile, had not even risen to receive this person. He motioned to him to be seated on a stool near the door; and after a few moments' silence, during which he seemed to be pursuing a previous meditation, he said to him in a somewhat patronizing tone, 'Good-day, Maître Jacques.'

'Greetings, maître,' replied the man in black.

'Well,' resumed the archdeacon, after another silence, which Maître Jacques took good care not to break, 'are you succeeding?'

'Alas! Maître,' said the other with a sorrowful smile; 'I keep on blowing. Plenty of ashes, but not a spark of gold.'

Dom Claude made a gesture of impatience.

'I was not talking of that, Maître Jacques Charmolue, but of the trial of your magician – is it not Marc Cenaine that you call him? – the butler of the Court of Accounts? Does he confess his sorcery? Have you been successful with the torture?'

'Alas, no!' replied Maître Jacques, still with his sad smile, 'we have not that consolation. That man is a stone; we might boil him at the pig-market before he would say anything. However, we spare no pains to get at the truth. He has already every joint dislocated. But all to no avail.'

'You have found nothing further in his house?'

'I'faith, yes,' said Maître Jacques, fumbling in his pouch; 'this parchment. There are words in it which we do not understand. Monsieur the criminal advocate, Philippe Lheuiler, knows, however, a little Hebrew, which he learned in that affair of the Jews of the Kantersten street, at Brussels. By-the-way, I was on the point of forgetting! When doth it please you that I shall apprehend the little sorceress?'

'What sorceress?'

'That gypsy-girl, you know, who comes and dances every day on the Parvis, in spite of the official's prohibition. She has a goat with devil's horns, which is possessed; it reads and writes, understands mathematics like Picatrix, and would suffice to hang all Bohemia. The prosecution is all ready; 'twill soon be got through with. A pretty creature, I warrant on my soul, that dancer – the handsomest black eyes! – two Egyptian carbuncles! When shall we begin?'

The archdeacon was excessively pale.

'I will let you know,' he stammered, in a voice scarcely articulate; then he resumed with an effort, 'Look you to Marc Cenaine.'

'Never fear,' said Charmolue, smiling; 'when I get back I'll have him buckled on the bed of leather again. The torture of the wheel! That is the best we have; he shall take a turn at that.'

They talked for some time on alchemy, then Dom Claude, fearing some prank of Jehan, reminded his worthy disciple that they had some figures on the portal to study together; and they both quitted the cell, with an exclamation from the student who began seriously to fear that his knees would bear the mark of his chin.

6

'*Te Deum laudamus!*' (We praise thee, O God!) exclaimed Master Jehan, issuing from his hole, 'the two screech-owls are gone at last. Whew! let me get down and take the big brother's purse to convert all these coins into bottles.'

He cast a glance of tenderness and admiration into the precious pouch; adjusted his dress; rubbed up his boots; dusted his poor furred sleeves, all gray with ashes; whistled an air; cut a caper; looked around to see if there was anything else in the cell that he could take; scraped up here and there from the furnace some amulet of glassware by way of trinket to give to Isabeau la Thierrye; finally pushed open the door which his brother had left unfastened as a last indulgence, and which he in turn left open as a last piece of mischief; and descended the winding stairs, skipping like a bird.

In the midst of the darkness of the spiral way he elbowed something, which drew aside with a growl. He presumed that it was Quasimodo; and it struck him as so droll that he descended the rest of the stairs holding his sides with laughter, and was still laughing when he got out into the Square.

He advanced a few steps, and caught sight of the two screech-owls, that is to say, Dom Claude and Maître Jacques Charmolue, contemplating one of the carvings on the portal.

At that moment he heard a powerful and sonorous voice behind him pour forth a formidable volley of oaths.

'My life for it,' exclaimed Jehan; 'that can be none other than my friend Captain Phœbus.'

This name of Phœbus reached the ears of the archdeacon just as he was explaining to the king's attorney the dragon hiding his tail in a bath from whence issued smoke and a king's head. Dom Claude started, stopped short, to the great astonishment of Charmolue, turned round, and saw his brother Jehan accosting a tall officer at the door of the Gondelaurier mansion.

It was, in fact, Captain Phœbus de Chateaupers. He was leaning against the corner of the house of his betrothed, and swearing like a Turk.

'By my faith, Captain Phœbus,' said Jehan, grasping his hand, 'you swear with a rare fancy.'

'Pardon me, good comrade Jehan,' cried Phœbus, shaking him by the hand; 'a galloping horse cannot stop short. Now, I was swearing at full gallop. I've just left those silly women, and when

I come away I always find my throat full of curses; I must spit them out or strangle – blood and thunder!'

'Will you come and drink?' asked the student.

This proposal calmed the captain.

'I fain would, but I have no money.'

'But I have.'

'Nonsense! let's see it.'

Jehan displayed the pouch before the captain's eyes with dignity and simplicity. Meanwhile, the archdeacon had approached them, and halted a few paces distant, watching them both without their noticing him, so absorbed were they in looking at the pouch.

Phœbus counted the coins; and, turning with solemn look toward Jehan, 'Know you, Jehan,' said he, 'that here are three and twenty Paris pence? Whom did you rifle last night in Rue Coupe-Gueule (Cut-gullet)?'

Jehan flung back his blond, curly head, and said, half closing his eyes disdainfully, 'One may have a brother who is an archdeacon and a simpleton!'

The two friends set out toward Pomme d'Eve.

The archdeacon followed them, haggard and gloomy. Was this the Phœbus whose accursed name, ever since his interview with Gringoire, had been mingled with all his thoughts? He knew not; but it was at least a Phœbus; and that magic name was sufficient inducement for the archdeacon to follow the two heedless comrades with stealthy step, listening to their words and observing their slightest gestures with anxious attention.

They talked of duels, wenches, flagons and frolics.

At the turn of a street, the sound of a tambourine reached them from a neighboring crossway. Dom Claude heard the officer say to the student, 'Thunder! let us hasten our steps.'

'Why, Phœbus?'

'I am afraid lest the gypsy will see me.'

'What gypsy?'

'The little one with a goat.'

'La 'Smeralda?'

'The same, Jehan. I always forget her devil of a name. Let us make haste; she will recognize me, and I would not wish that girl to accost me in the streets.'

'Are you then acquainted with her, Phœbus?'

Here the archdeacon saw Phœbus chuckle, stoop to Jehan's ear, and whisper a few words in it; Phœbus then burst into a laugh, and tossed his head with a triumphant air.

'For a truth?' said Jehan.

'On my soul!' said Phœbus.

'This evening?'

'This evening!'

'Are you sure she will come?'

'Are you a fool, Jehan? Can there ever be any doubt in such matters?'

'Captain Phœbus, you are a lucky soldier.'

The archdeacon overheard all this conversation. His teeth chattered; a visible shiver ran through his whole body. He stopped a moment, leaned against a post like a drunken man, then followed in the track of two jolly scamps.

7

The celebrated wine-shop of La Pomme d'Eve was a very spacious but very low room on the ground floor, with an arched roof, the central spring of which rested on a huge wooden pillar, painted yellow.

Night was falling; the street was dark; the wine-shop, full of candles, flamed from afar like a forge in the darkness; the noise of glasses and feasting, of oaths and quarrels, could be heard through the broken panes. Through the mist which the heat of the room spread over the front casement, a multitude of swarming figures could be seen confusedly; and from time to time a burst of noisy laughter broke forth from it.

One man, however, paced imperturbably back and forth in front of the noisy tavern, looking at it incessantly, and going no farther from it than a pikeman from his sentry-box. He was cloaked up to the nose. This cloak he had just bought of the old clothes man near La Pomme d'Eve, doubtless to protect himself from the cold of a March night – perhaps also to conceal his costume. From time to time he paused before the dim lattice-leaded casement, listened, looked and stamped his foot.

At length the tavern-door opened. It was for this that he seemed to have been waiting. Two tipplers came out. The ray of light which escaped from the door cast a glow for a moment on their jovial faces. The man in the cloak stationed himself under a porch on the other side of the street.

'Thunder and guns!' said one of the two drinkers, ' 'tis on the stroke of seven – the hour of my appointed meeting!'

'I tell you,' repeated his companion, with a thick utterance, 'that I don't live in the Rue des Mauvaises Paroles (bad words) – *Indignus qui inter mala verba habitat.* (Unworthy he who lives among bad words). I lodge in the Rue Jean Pain Mollet –

89

in vico Joannis Pain Mollet – and you are more horned than a unicorn if you say the contrary.

'Jehan, my friend, you are drunk,' said the other.

The reader has no doubt already recognized our two worthy friends, the captain and the student. The man who was watching them in the dark appeared also to have recognized them; for he followed with slow steps all the zigzags which the reeling student forced the captain to describe, who, being a more seasoned drinker, had retained all his self-possession. By listening attentively, the man in the cloak was enabled to catch the whole of the following interesting conversation:

'*Corbacque!* (Body o' Bacchus!) try to walk straight, master bachelor; you know that I must leave you. It is seven o'clock. I have to meet a woman. By the way, Jehan, have you no money left? You know I have promised to meet that little girl at the end of the Pont Saint Michel; that I can take her nowhere but to La Falourdel's, the old crone of the bridge, and that I must pay for the room. The white-whiskered old jade will give me no credit. Jehan, for pity's sake, have we drunk up the whole of the priest's pouch? Haven't you a penny left?'

'The consciousness of having spent the other hours well is a just and savory sauce for the table.'

'Belly and guts! a truce to your gibberish. Tell me – you devil of a Jehan – have you any coin left? Give it me, by heaven! or I'll search you all over, were you as leprous as Job, and as mangy as Cæsar.'

'Sir, the Rue Galiache is a street with the Rue de la Verrerie at one end of it, and the Rue de la Tixeranderie at the other.'

'Well, scholar of Antichrist, mayst thou be strangled with the guts of thy mother!' exclaimed Phœbus; and he gave the tipsy student a rough push, which sent him reeling against a wall, whence he fell gently upon the pavement of Philip Augustus.

'So much the worse for thee, if the devil's cart picks thee up as it goes by,' said he to the poor, sleeping clerk; and he went his way.

The man in the cloak ceased following him and stopped for a moment beside the prostrate student, as if agitated by indecision; then heaving a deep sigh, he continued to follow the captain.

On turning into the Rue Saint André des Arcs, Captain Phœbus perceived that someone was following him. As he accidentally glanced behind him, he saw a sort of shadow creeping behind him along the walls. He stopped – it stopped; he went on – the shadow went on again also. This, however, gave him very little concern. 'Ah! bah!' said he to himself, 'I have not a penny about me.'

In front of the Collège d'Autun he came to a halt. The street was utterly deserted. As he was retagging nonchalantly his doublet with his head thrown back, he saw the shadow approaching him slowly — so slowly that he had full time to observe that this shadow had a cloak and a hat. When it had come up to him, it stopped, and remained as motionless as statue. But it riveted upon Phœbus two intent eyes, glaring with that vague light which issues at night from those of a cat.

The captain was brave, and would have cared little for a robber with a rapier in his hand. But this walking statue, this petrified man, made his blood run cold. At that time there were certain strange rumors afloat about a spectre monk, a nocturnal prowler about the streets of Paris in the night-time, and they now came confusedly to his mind. He stood stupefied for a few moments, then finally broke silence with a laugh.

'Sir,' said he, 'if you be a thief, as I hope is the case, you're just now for all the world like a heron attacking a walnut-shell. My dear fellow, I am the son of a ruined family. Try your hand hard by here. In the chapel of this college there's some wood of the true cross, set in silver.'

The hand of the shadow came forth from under its cloak, and descended upon the arm of Phœbus with the force of an eagle's grip; at the same time the shadow spoke:

'Captain Phœbus de Chateaupers!'

'What, the devil!' said Phœbus; 'you know my name?'

'I know not your name alone,' returned the man in the cloak, with his sepulchral voice; 'but I know that you have an appointment this evening.'

'Yes,' answered Phœbus, in amazement.

'At seven o'clock.'

'In a quarter of an hour.'

'At the Falourdel's.'

'Exactly so.'

'Impious man!' muttered the spectre. 'With a woman?'

'La 'Smeralda,' said Phœbus gaily, all his heedlessness having gradually returned to him.

At this name the shadow's grasp shook Phœbus's arm furiously.

'Captain Phœbus de Chateaupers, thou liest!'

Anyone who could have seen, at that moment, the captain's inflamed countenance — his leap backwards, so violent that it disengaged him from the clutch which held him — the haughty mien with which he clapped his hand on his sword-hilt — and, in the presence of this wrath, the sullen stillness of the man in the cloak; anyone who could have beheld this would have been frightened.

'Christ and Satan!' cried the captain; 'that's a word that seldom assails the ear of a Chateaupers! Thou durst not repeat it.'

'Thou liest!' said the shadow coldly.

The captain ground his teeth. Spectre monk – phantom – superstitions – all were forgotten at that moment. He now saw nothing but a man and an insult. 'Ha, it is well!' spluttered he in a voice choking with rage. He drew his sword; then, stuttering, for anger as well as fear makes a man tremble – 'Here!' said he, 'on the spot! Come on! Swords! swords! Blood upon these stones!'

But the other did not stir. When he saw his adversary on guard, and ready to lunge, 'Captain Phœbus,' said he, and his voice quivered with bitterness, 'you forget your assignation.'

The fits of rage of such men as Phœbus are like boiling milk, whose ebullition is calmed by a drop of cold water. These few words brought down the point of the sword which glittered in the captain's hand.

'Captain,' continued the man, 'tomorrow – the day after tomorrow – a month hence – ten years hence – you will find me quite ready to cut your throat. But first go to your assignation.'

'Sir,' answered Phœbus, with some embarrassment, 'gramercy for your courtesy. It will, in truth, be time enough tomorrow to chop up father Adam's doublet into slashes and buttonholes. I will, therefore, betake myself to my appointment. It is for the hour of seven, as you know.' Here Phœbus scratched his ear. 'Ah! by my halidom! I forgot! I have not a penny to pay the price of the garret, and the old hag will want to be paid beforehand; she distrusts me.'

'Here is the wherewithal to pay.'

Phœbus felt the stranger's cold hand slip into his a large coin. He could not help taking the money, and grasping the hand. 'God's truth!' he exclaimed, 'but you're a good fellow!'

'One condition,' said the man. 'Prove to me that I was wrong, and that you spoke truth. Hide me in some corner whence I may see whether this woman be really she whose name you uttered.'

'Oh,' replied Phœbus, ' 'tis all one to me. We will take the Saint Martha chamber. You can see at your ease from the kennel hard by.'

'Come, then,' rejoined the shadow.

'At your service,' said the captain. 'I know not indeed whether you be not Messer Diabolus. But let us be good friends tonight; tomorrow I'll pay you all debts, of purse and of sword.'

They set out again at a rapid pace. In a few minutes the sound of the river below apprised them that they were upon the bridge of Saint Michel, then covered with houses.

'I will first let you in,' said Phœbus to his companion; 'then I will go fetch the wench who was to wait for me near the Petit-Châtelet.'

That companion made no reply; since they had been walking side by side, he had not uttered a word. Phœbus stopped before a low door and knocked loudly. A light appeared through the cracks of the door. 'Who's there?' cried a mumbling voice.

'By the body! by the belly! by the head of God!' answered the captain.

The door opened instantly, and revealed to the newcomers an old woman and an old lamp, both of which trembled. The old woman was bent double – dressed in rags – with a shaking head, pierced by two small eyes, and coiffed with a dish clout – wrinkled everywhere, on hands and face and neck – her lips receding under her gums – and all round her mouth she had tufts of white hair, which gave her the whiskered and demure look of a cat.

The interior of the hovel was no less dilapidated than herself; the walls were of plaster; black rafters ran across the ceiling; a dismantled fireplace; cobwebs in every corner; in the middle of the room a tottering company of maimed stools and tables; a dirty child played in the ash-heap; and at the farther end a staircase, or rather a wooden ladder, led to a trap-door in the ceiling.

As he entered this den, Phœbus's mysterious companion drew his cloak up to his eyes. Meanwhile, the captain, swearing like a Turk, hastened 'to make the sun flash from a crownpiece,' as saith our admirable Régnier.

'The Saint Martha room,' said he.

The old woman addressed him as monseigneur, and deposited the crown in a drawer. It was the coin which the man in the black cloak had given Phœbus. While her back was turned, the ragged, disheveled little boy, who was playing in the ashes, went slyly to the drawer, abstracted the crown-piece, and put in its place a dry leaf which he had plucked from a fagot.

The hag beckoned to the two gentlemen, as she called them, to follow her, and ascended the ladder before them. On reaching the upper story, she placed her lamp upon a chest; and Phœbus, like a frequenter of the house, opened the door of a dark closet. 'Go in there, my dear fellow,' said he to his companion. The man in the cloak complied without uttering a word; the door closed upon him; he heard Phœbus bolt it, and, a moment afterward, go downstairs again with the old woman. The light had disappeared.

8

Claude Frollo (for we presume that the reader, more clever than Phœbus, has seen in this whole adventure no other spectre monk that the archdeacon himself) groped about for some moments in the dark hole into which the captain had bolted him. It was one of those nooks such as architects sometimes leave at the junction of the roof and the outer wall. The vertical section of this kennel, as Phœbus had so aptly termed it, would have made a triangle. There was neither window nor skylight, and the pitch of the roof prevented one from standing upright. Claude, therefore, crouched down in the dust and plaster which crumbled beneath him. His head was burning. Feeling about him with his hands, he found on the floor a bit of broken glass, which he pressed to his brow, its coolness affording him some relief.

He had been waiting a quarter of an hour; it seemed to him that he had grown a century older. All at once he heard the wooden staircase creak; someone was coming up. The trap-door opened once more; light reappeared. In the worm-eaten door of his nook there was a crack of considerable width; to this he glued his face. Thus he could see all that went on in the adjoining chamber. The cat-faced old woman appeared first through the trap-door with lamp in hand; then Phœbus, twirling his mustache; then a third person, that lovely, graceful creature, La Esmeralda. The priest beheld her rise from below like a dazzling apparition. Claude trembled; a cloud spread over his eyes; his pulse beat violently; everything swam before him; he no longer saw or heard anything.

When he came to himself again, Phœbus and Esmeralda were alone, seated on the wooden chest, beside the lamp, whose light revealed to the archdeacon's eyes their two youthful figures, and a miserable pallet at the farther end of the garret.

The young girl was blushing, confused, palpitating. Her long drooping lashes shaded her glowing cheeks. The face of the officer, to which she dared not lift her eyes, was radiant. Mechanically, and with a charming air of embarrassment, she traced with the tip of her finger meaningless lines upon the bench, and watched her finger. Her feet were not visible, for the little goat was nestling upon them.

Dom Claude could only hear with great difficulty what they

said to each other, through the humming of the blood that was boiling in his temples.

'Oh!' said the young girl, without lifting her eyes, 'despise me not, Monseigneur Phœbus; I feel that what I am doing is wrong.'

'Despise you, my pretty dear,' replied the officer with a consequential and modish air of gallantry; 'despise you, good lack! and why should I?'

'For having accompanied you.'

'On that score, my charmer, we don't at all agree. I ought not only to despise you, but to hate you.'

The young girl looked at him in affright: 'Hate me! What, then, have I done?'

'For requiring so much solicitation.'

'Alas!' said she, ''tis because I am breaking a vow – I shall never find my parents – the amulet will lose its virtue; but what then? What need have I for father and mother now?'

Esmeralda remained silent for a moment; then a tear fell from her eye, a sigh from her lips, and she said, 'Oh, monseigneur, I love you.'

Such a perfume of chastity, such a charm of virtue, surrounded the young girl that Phœbus did not feel quite at his ease with her. These words, however, emboldened him. 'You love me!' said he with rapture, and he threw his arm round the gypsy's waist. He had only been waiting for this opportunity.

The priest saw him, and tested with the tip of his finger the point of a dagger concealed in his breast.

'Phœbus,' continued the Bohemian, gently disengaging her waist from the tenacious hands of the captain, 'you are good – you are generous – you are handsome – you have saved me – me, who am but a poor gypsy foundling. I have long dreamed of an officer who should save my life. It was of you that I dreamed, before I knew you, my Phœbus. The officer of my dream had a beautiful uniform like yours, a grand air, a sword. Your name is Phœbus – 'tis a beautiful name. I love your name, I love your sword. Draw your sword, Phœbus, that I may see it.'

'Child!' said the captain; and he unsheathed his rapier with a smile.

The gypsy-girl looked at the hilt, then at the blade; examined with adorable curiosity the cypher upon the guard, and kissed the weapon, saying, 'You are the sword of a brave man. I love my captain.'

Phœbus again took advantage of the situation to imprint on her lovely bent neck a kiss which made the girl start up as red as a cherry. It made the priest grind his teeth in the darkness.

'Hark you, my dear . . .'

The gypsy gave him a few little taps on the lips with her pretty hand with a childish playfulness, full of gaiety and grace.

'No, no, I will not listen. Do you love me? I want you to tell me if you love me.'

'Do I love thee, angel of my life?' cried the captain, half kneeling before her. 'My body, my blood, my soul – all are thine – all are for thee. I love thee, and have never loved any but thee.'

The captain had repeated this phrase so many times, on many similar occasions, that he delivered it all in a breath, and without making a single mistake. At this impassioned declaration, the gypsy raised to the dingy ceiling a look full of angelic happiness. 'Oh!' murmured she, 'this is the moment when one should die!'

Phœbus thought 'the moment' a good one to steal another kiss, which tortured the wretched archdeacon in his lair.

'Die!' cried the amorous captain; 'what are you talking of, my lovely angel? 'Tis the time to live. Die at the beginning of so sweet a thing! That would not do. Listen, my dear Similar – Esmenarda – Your pardon! but you have so prodigiously Saracen a name that I never can get it straight; I get entangled in it like a briar.'

'Good heavens!' said the poor girl, 'and I thought my name pretty because of its singularity! But, since it displeases you, I would that I were called Goton.'

'Ah! do not weep for such a trifle, my graceful maid; 'tis a name to which one must get used, that is all. When once I know it by heart, 'twill come ready enough. So hark ye, my dear Similar. I adore you passionately; I love you so that 'tis really marvelous. I know a little girl that's bursting with rage about it.'

For some moments the young girl, absorbed in her pleasing reflections, had been dreaming to the sound of his voice, without heeding the meaning of his words.

'Oh, how happy you will be!' continued the captain, and at the same time he gently unbuckled the gypsy's girdle.

'What are you doing?' she said quickly. This 'act of violence' had roused her from her reverie.

'Nothing,' answered Phœbus.

The captain, emboldened by her gentleness, clasped her waist without her making any resistance; then began softly to unlace the poor child's bodice, and so greatly disarranged her neckerchief that the panting priest beheld the gypsy's lovely shoulder emerge from the gauze, round and dusky like the moon rising through the mists of the horizon.

The young girl let Phœbus have his way. She seemed unconscious of what he was doing. The bold captain's eyes sparkled.

All at once she turned towards him.

'Phœbus,' said she, with an expression of infinite love, 'instruct me in thy religion.'

'My religion!' cried the captain, bursting into a laugh. 'I instruct you in my religion. Blood and thunder! what do you want with my religion?'

'That we may be married,' she replied.

The captain's face assumed a mingled expression of surprise, disdain, carelessness and licentious passion.

'Bah,' said he, 'why should one marry?'

The gypsy turned pale, and her head drooped sadly on her breast.

'My sweet love,' resumed Phœbus, tenderly, 'what are all these foolish ideas? Marriage is a grand affair, to be sure. Is any one less loving for not having spouted Latin in a priest's shop?'

While speaking thus in his softest tone, he approached extremely near the gypsy-girl; his caressing hands resumed their place around the lithe, slender waist. His eyes kindled more and more.

Dom Claude meanwhile saw all from his hiding-place. Its door was made of decayed planks, leaving between them ample passage for his look of a bird of prey. This brown-skinned, broad-shouldered priest hitherto condemned to the austere virginity of the cloister, was quivering and boiling in the presence of this night-scene of love and voluptuousness. The young and lovely girl, her garments in disorder, abandoning herself to the ardent young man, seemed to infuse molten lead into his veins. An extraordinary agitation shook him; his eyes sought with lustful desire to penetrate beneath all those unfastened pins.

Suddenly, with a rapid motion, Phœbus snatched off the gypsy's neckerchief. The poor girl, who had remained pale and dreamy, started up as if suddenly awakened; she hastily drew back from the enterprising officer; and casting a glance at her bare neck and shoulders, blushing, confused, and mute with shame, she crossed her two lovely arms upon her breasts to hide them.

But the captain's action had exposed the mysterious amulet which she wore about her neck.

'What is that?' said he, seizing this pretext to approach once more the beautiful creature whom he had just alarmed.

'Touch it not,' she replied quickly; ' 'tis my protector. It will help me to find my family again, if I remain worthy to do so. Oh, leave me, sir! My mother! my poor mother! my mother! where art thou? Come to my rescue! Have pity, Captain Phœbus; give me back my neckerchief.'

Phœbus drew back, and said coldly:

'Oh, young lady, I see plainly that you do not love me.'

'Not love him!' exclaimed the unhappy child, and at the same time clinging to the captain and drawing him to a seat by her side. 'Not love thee, my Phœbus? What art thou saying, wicked man, to rend my heart? Oh, come – take me – take all – do with me as thou wilt – I am thine. What matters the amulet to me now? What matters my mother to me now? My soul, my life, my body, my person, all is one thing – which is thine, my captain. Here, Phœbus, all this belongs to thee. Only love me. We gypsy-girls need nothing more – air and love.'

So saying, she threw her arms around the officer's neck; she looked up at him imploringly and smiled through her tears. Her delicate neck rubbed against his cloth doublet with its rough embroidery. She twisted her beautiful, half-naked limbs around his knees. The intoxicated captain pressed his burning lips to those lovely African shoulders.

All at once, above the head of Phœbus, she beheld another head – a green, livid, convulsed face, with the look of a lost soul; beside this face there was a hand which held a dagger. It was the face and hand of the priest; he had broken open the door, and he was there. Phœbus could not see him. The young girl was motionless, frozen mute at the frightful apparition.

She could not even utter a cry. She saw the poniard descend upon Phœbus, and rise again reeking.

'Malediction!' said the captain, and he fell.

She fainted.

As her eyes closed, as all consciousness left her, she thought she felt a fiery touch upon her lips, a kiss more burning than the executioner's branding-iron.

When she recovered her senses, she was surrounded by soldiers of the watch; they were carrying off the captain weltering in his blood; the priest had disappeared; the window at the back of the room, looking upon the river, was wide open; they picked up a cloak which they supposed to belong to the officer, and she heard them saying around her:

' 'Tis a sorceress who has stabbed a captain.'

BOOK SIX

1

Gringoire and the whole Court of Miracles were in a state of terrible anxiety. For a whole month no one knew what had become of La Esmeralda, which sorely grieved the Duke of Egypt and his friends the vagrants; nor what had become of her goat, which redoubled Gringoire's sorrow. One night the gypsy had disappeared; and since that time had given no signs of life. All search had proved fruitless.

He could not explain her disappearance. It was a great grief to him. He would have grown thinner upon it, had that been possible. He had forgotten everything else, even to his literary pursuits.

One day, as he was passing sadly before the Criminal Tournelle, he perceived a crowd at one of the doors of the Palace of Justice.

'What is there?' he inquired of a young man who was coming out.

'I know not, sir,' replied the young man. ' 'Tis said a woman is being tried for the murder of a man-at-arms. As there seems to be something of sorcery in the business, the bishop and the judge of the Bishop's Court have interposed in the cause; and my brother, the archdeacon of Josas, can think of nothing else. Now, I wished to speak to him; but could not get at him for the crowd – which vexes me mightily, for I am in need of money.'

'Alas! sir,' said Gringoire, 'I would I could lend you some; but, though my breeches are in holes, it's not from the weight of crown-pieces.'

He dared not tell the young man that he knew his brother, the archdeacon, to whom he had not returned since the scene in the church – a negligence which embarrassed him.

The student went his way, and Gringoire followed the crowd going up the staircase of the Great Hall.

The hall was huge and ill-lighted, which latter circumstance made it seeme still larger. The day was declining; the high, pointed windows admitted but a faint ray of light. There were already several candles lighted here and there upon tables, and glimmering over the heads of the clerks bending over musty documents. The front of the hall was occupied by the crowd; to the right and left were lawyers in their robes seated at tables; at the farther end, upon a raised platform, were a number of judges, the last rows of whom were lost in the darkness – with immovable and sinister-looking faces.

'My lords,' an old woman in the middle of the hall was saying, whose face was so concealed beneath her garments that she might have been taken for a walking bundle of rags – 'my lords, the thing is as true as it is true that my name it Falourdel, and that for forty years I have lived on the Pont Saint Michel, and paid regularly my rent, dues and quit-rent.

'One evening I was spinning at my wheel, when there comes a knock at my door. I ask who is there. Some one swears. I open the door. Two men enter – one in black, with a handsome officer. Of the one in black nothing could be seen but his eyes – two coals of fire. All the rest was cloak and hat. And so they say to me. "The Saint Martha room." 'Tis my upper chamber, my lords – my best. They give me a crown. I lock the crown in my drawer, and I say, "This shall go to buy tripe tomorrow at the Gloriette shambles." We go up-stairs. On reaching the upper room, and while my back was turned, the black man disappears. This startled me a bit. The officer, who was as handsome as a great lord, goes down-stairs with me. He leaves the house. In about time enough to spin a quarter of a bobbin, he comes back again with a beautiful young girl – a doll who would have shone like the sun had her hair been dressed. She had with her a goat, a great he-goat, whether black or white I no longer remember. That set me to thinking. The girl – that was no concern of mine – but the goat! I don't like those animals; they have a beard and horns – it is like a man; and then they smack of the witches' sabbath. However, I said nothing. I had the crown-piece. I show the captain and the girl into the upstairs room, and leave them alone – that is to say, with the goat. I go down and get to my spinning again. I must tell you that my house has a ground-floor and a floor above; the back of it looks upon the river, like the other houses on the bridge, and the windows, both of the ground-floor and of the chamber, upon the water. Well, as I was saying, I had got to my spinning. I know not why I fell to thinking of the spectre monk whom the goat had put into my head again – and then the beautiful girl was rather strangely tricked out. All at once I hear a cry overhead, and something falls on the floor, and the window opens. I run to mine, which is beneath it, and I see a dark mass drop past my eyes into the water. It was a phantom clad like a priest. The moon was shining; I saw it quite plainly. It was swimming toward the City. Then, all of a tremble, I call the watch. The

100

gentlemen of the police come in; and being merry, not knowing at first what was the matter, they fell to beating me. I explained to them. We got upstairs, and what do we find? My poor chamber all blood – the captain stretched out at full length with a dagger in his neck – the girl pretending to be dead – and the goat all in a fright. But wait. The worst is, that on the next day, when I went to get the crown to buy tripe, I found a withered leaf in its place.'

The old woman ceased. A murmur of horror ran through the audience.

The magistrate now rose.

'Silence,' said he; 'I beg you, gentlemen, to bear in mind that a poniard was found on the accused. Woman Falourdel, have you brought the leaf into which the crown was changed that the demon gave you?'

'Yes, monseigneur,' answered she; 'I found it. Here it is.'

An usher of the court handed the withered leaf to the magistrate, who with a doleful shake of the head, passed it on to the president, who gave it to the king's attorney in the ecclesiastical court; and thus it made the circuit of the hall.

'I will recall to these gentlemen that in the deposition taken at his bedside, the murdered officer, while admitting that he had a confused idea, at the moment when the black man accosted him, that it might be the spectre monk, added that the phantom had eagerly pressed him to keep his appointment with the prisoner; and on his, the captain's, observing that he was without money, he had given him the crown which the said Phœbus had paid La Falourdel. Hence, the crown is a coin from hell.'

At that name the accused sprang up; her head rose above the throng. Gringoire, aghast, recognized Esmeralda.

She was pale; her hair, once so gracefully plaited and spangled with sequins, hung in disorder; her lips were livid; her hollow eyes were terrible. Alas!

'Phœbus!' said she, wildly; 'where is he? Oh, messeigneurs! before you kill me, tell me, for pity's sake, whether he yet lives!'

'Be silent, woman,' answered the president; 'that is no concern of ours.'

'Oh, have mercy! tell me if he is alive,' continued she, clasping her beautiful, emaciated hands; and her chains were heard as they brushed along her dress.

'Well,' said the king's advocate roughly, 'he is dying. Does that content you?'

The wretched girl fell back on her seat, speechless, tearless, white as a wax figure.

'Usher, bring in the second accused.'

All eyes were now turned toward a small door, which opened, and, to the great agitation of Gringoire, made way for a pretty goat with gilded hoofs and horns. The dainty creature paused for a moment on the threshold, stretching out its neck as though, perched on the summit of a rock, it had before its eyes a vast horizon. All at once it caught sight of the gypsy-girl; and leaping over the table and a registrar's head in two bounds it was at her knees. It then rolled gracefully on its mistress's feet, begging for a word or a caress; but the prisoner remained motionless, and poor Djali itself obtained not a glance.

'If it please you, gentlemen, we will proceed to the examination of the goat.'

The king's attorney in the ecclesiastical court cried out: 'If the demon which possesses this goat, and which has resisted all exorcisms, persist in its deeds of witchcraft — if he alarm the court with them — we warn him that we shall be obliged to put in requisition against it the gibbet or the stake.'

Gringoire broke out into a cold perspiration. Charmolue took from a table the gypsy's tambourine, and, presenting it in a certain manner to the goat, he asked the latter:

'What o'clock is it?'

The goat looked at him with an intelligent eye, raised her gilt foot, and struck seven blows. It was indeed seven o'clock. A movement of terror ran through the crowd.

Gringoire could no longer contain himself.

'She'll be her own ruin,' cried he aloud; 'you see that she knows not what she is doing!'

'Silence among the louts at the end of the hall!' said the bailiff, sharply.

Jacques Charmolue, by means of the same manoeuvres with the tambourine, made the goat perform several other tricks connected with the day of the month, the month of the year, etc, which the reader has already witnessed.

It was still worse when, the king's attorney having emptied on the floor a certain leathern bag full of detached letters which Djali wore about her neck, they beheld the goat sort out with its foot from among the scattered alphabet the fatal name: *Phœbus.* The sorcery of which the captain had been the victim seemed unanswerably proved; and, in the eyes of all, the gypsy-girl, that enchanting dancer, who had so often dazzled the passers-by with her grace, was no longer anything but a frightful vampire.

However, she gave no sign of life; neither the graceful evolutions of Djali, nor the threats of the magistrates, nor the muttered imprecations of the audience – nothing seemed to reach her ear.

In order to arouse her, a sergeant was obliged to shake her unmercifully, while the president solemnly raised his voice:

'Girl, you are of Bohemian race, addicted to deeds of witchcraft. You, in complicity with the bewitched goat, implicated in the charge, did, on the night of the 29th of March last, wound and poniard, in concert with the powers of darkness, by the aid of charms and spells, a captain of the king's archers, Phœbus de Chateaupers by name. Do you persist in denying it?'

'Do I deny it!' said she, in terrible accents; and she rose with flashing eyes.

The president continued bluntly:

'Then how do you explain the facts laid to your charge?'

She answered in a broken voice:

'I have already told you I know not. It is a priest – a priest whom I do not know – an infernal priest, who pursues me!'

'Just so,' replied the judge; 'the spectre monk!'

'Oh, gentlemen, have pity! I am only a poor girl . . .'

Maître Jacques Charmolue interposed sweetly – 'In view of the sad obstinacy of the accused, I demand the application of the torture.'

'Granted,' said the president.

A shudder ran through the whole frame of the wretched girl. She rose, however, at the order of the halberdiers, and walked with a tolerably firm step, preceded by Charmolue and the priests of the officiality, between two rows of halberds, toward a false door, which suddenly opened and closed again behind her.

2

After ascending and descending some steps in passages so dark that they were lighted in broad day by lamps, Esmeralda, still surrounded by her lugubrious attendants, was pushed forward by the sergeants of the Palace into a room of sinister aspect. There are no windows to this cellar; no other opening than the entrance, which was low and closed by an enormous iron door. Nevertheless, light was not lacking. A furnace had been constructed in the thickness of the wall; a large fire was lighted in it, which filled the vault with its crimson reflection. By the light which it cast, the prisoner saw all about the room frightful instruments whose use she did not understand. In the middle was a leathern mattress laid almost flat upon the ground, over which hung a thong with a buckle fastened to a copper ring which a flat-nosed monster carved in the keystone of the vault held between his teeth. Tongs, pincers, large plowshares, were heaped inside the furnace, and were heating red-hot, promiscuously upon the burning coals. The blood-red glow of the furnace illuminated in the chamber only a confused mass of horrible things.

This was called simply the question chamber.

Upon the bed was seated carelessly Pierrat Torterue, the official torturer. His underlings, two square-faced gnomes, with leathern aprons and tarpaulin coats, were turning about the irons on the coals.

In vain the poor girl called up all her courage; on entering this room she was seized with horror.

The sergeants of the bailiff of the Palace ranged themselves on one side; the priests of the Bishop's Court on the other. A clerk and a table with writing materials were in one corner.

Maître Jacques Charmolue approached the gypsy with a very sweet smile.

'My dear child,' said he, 'do you still persist in your denial?'

'Yes,' she replied in a faint voice.

'In that case,' resumed Charmolue, 'it will be our painful duty to question you more urgently than we should otherwise wish. Have the goodness to sit down on this bed.'

Meanwhile, La Esmeralda remained standing. That leathern bed, on which so many poor wretches had writhed, frightened her. Terror froze her very marrow; there she stood bewildered and stupefied. At a sign from Charmolue, the two assistants laid hold of her and seated her on the bed. They did her no harm; but when those men touched her – when that leather touched her – she felt all her blood flow back to her heart.

She shuddered.

'Mademoiselle,' resumed the fawning voice of the attorney of the ecclesiastical court, 'for the third time, do you persist in denying the facts of which you are accused?'

This time she could only make a sign with her head; her voice failed her.

'You persist?' said Jacques Charmolue. 'Then it grieves me deeply, but I must fulfil the duty of my office.'

'Monsieur, the king's procurator,' said Pierrat gruffly, 'with what shall we begin?'

Charmolue hesitated a moment, with the doubtful grimace of a poet seeking rhyme.

'With the boot,' said he at last.

The unfortunate creature felt herself so utterly abandoned by

God and man that her head fell upon her breast like a thing inert, destitute of all strength.

The torturer and the doctor approached her both at once. The two assistants began rummaging in their hideous arsenal.

At the sound of those frightful irons the unfortunate girl quivered like a dead frog which is being galvanized. 'Oh,' murmured she, so low that no one heard her, 'Oh, my Phœbus!' She then relapsed into her former immobility and petrified silence.

Meanwhile, the horny hands of Pierrat Torterue's assistants had brutally bared that beautiful leg, that little foot, which had so often delighted the by-standers with their grace and loveliness in the streets of Paris.

Presently the poor girl saw through the mist which spread before her eyes the 'boot' approach; soon she saw her foot, encased between the iron-bound boards, disappear in the frightful apparatus. Then terror restored her strength.

'Take off that,' she cried frantically; and starting up all disheveled, 'Mercy!'

She sprang from the bed to fling herself at the feet of the king's attorney; but her leg was held fast in the heavy block of oak and iron-work, and she sank upon the boot more helpless than a bee with a leaden weight upon its wings.

At a sign from Charmolue she was replaced on the bed and two coarse hands fastened round her small waist the leathern strap which hung from the ceiling.

'For the last time, do you confess the facts of the charge?' asked Charmolue, with his imperturbable benignity.

'I am innocent.'

'Proceed,' said Charmolue to Pierrat. Pierrat turned the handle of the screw jack; the boot tightened, and the wretched victim uttered one of those horrible shrieks which can't be written in any human language.

'Stop,' said Charmolue to Pierrat.

'Do you confess?' said he to the gypsy.

'Everything!' cried the wretched girl. 'I confess! I confess! Mercy!'

She had not calculated her strength when she faced the torture.

'Humanity forces me to tell you,' observed the king's attorney, 'that, in confessing, you have only to look for death.'

'I hope so,' said she; and she sank back upon the leathern bed lifeless, bent double, suspended by the thong buckled round her waist.

Jacques Charmolue raised his voice:

'Clerk, write. Bohemian girl, you confess your participation in the love-feasts, witches' sabbaths and practices of hell, with wicked spirits, witches and hobgoblins? Answer.'

'Yes,' said she, so low that it was lost in a whisper.

'You confess to having seen the ram which Beelzebub causes to appear in the clouds to call together the witches' sabbath, and which is only seen by sorcerers?'

'Yes.'

'Lastly, you avow and confess having, with the assistance of the demon and of the phantom commonly called the spectre monk, on the night of the twenty-ninth of March last, murdered and assassinated a captain named Phœbus de Chateaupers?'

She raised her large staring eyes to the magistrate and replied, as if mechanically, without effort or emotion:

'Yes.'

It was evident that she was utterly broken.

'Write down, registrar,' said Charmolue; and addressing the torturers: 'Let the prisoner be unbound and taken back into court.'

3

When, pale and limping, she re-entered the court, a general hum of pleasure greeted her. The little goat, too, bleated with joy. She tried to run to her mistress, but they had tied her to the bench.

Night had quite set in. The candles, whose number had not been increased, gave so little light that the walls of the hall could not be seen. Darkness enveloped every object in a sort of mist. A few apathetic judges' faces were just visible. Opposite to them, at the extremity of the long hall, they could distinguish a vague white patch against the dark background. It was the accused.

She had dragged herself to her place. When Charmolue had magisterially installed himself in his, he sat down; then rose and said, without exhibiting too much of the self-complacency of success. 'The accused has confessed all.'

'Bohemian girl,' continued the president, 'you have confessed all your acts of sorcery, prostitution and assassination upon Phœbus de Chateaupers?'

Her heart was wrung. She was heard sobbing amid the darkness.

'Whatever you will,' answered she feebly; 'but kill me quickly.'

The question was put to the vote without leaving the hall. The judges nodded assent; they were in haste. Their capped heads were seen uncovered one after another in the dusk at the lugubrious question addressed to them in a low voice by the president. The poor accused seemed to be looking at them, but her bewildered eye no longer saw anything.

The clerk of the court began to write; then he handed the president a long scroll of parchment.

The unhappy girl then heard a stir among the people, the pikes clash and a chilling voice say:

'Bohemian girl, on such day as it shall please our lord the king, at the hour of noon, you shall be taken in a tumbrel, in your shift, barefoot, with a rope around your neck, before the great portal of Notre-Dame; and there you shall do penance with a wax torch of two pounds weight in your hand; and from thence you shall be taken to the Place de Grève, where you shall be hanged and strangled on the town gibbet, and likewise this, your goat; and you will pay to the Bishop's Court three lions of gold, in reparation of the crimes, by you committed and confessed, of sorcery, magic, debauchery and murder, upon the person of the sieur Phœbus de Chateaupers. So God have mercy on your soul!'

'Oh! 'tis a dream!' murmured she; and she felt rough hands bearing her away.

4

In the Middle Ages, when an edifice was complete, there was almost as much of it under the ground as above it. Unless built upon piles, like Notre-Dame, a palace, a fortress or a church had always a double bottom. In cathedrals it was, as it were, another subterranean cathedral, low, dark, mysterious, blind, mute, under the upper nave which was overflowing with light and resounding night and day with the music of bells and organs. Sometimes it was a sepulchre. In palaces and fortresses it was a prison; sometimes a sepulchre also, sometimes both together.

At the fortress of Saint Antoine, at the Palace of Justice of Paris, at the Louvre, these subterranean edifices were prisons. The storeys of these prisons, as they went deeper into the ground, grew narrower and darker. They formed so many zones, presenting various degrees of horror. These tunnel-like dungeons usually ended in a deep hole, shaped like the bottom of a tub, where society placed those condemned to death. When once a miserable human existence was there interred, then it only came forth to the gibbet or to the stake. Sometimes it rotted there; human justice called that *forgetting*.

It was in a dungeon hole of this kind, in the *oubliettes* excavated by Saint Louis in the *in pace* (prison in which monks were shut up for life) of the Tournelle, that – for fear of her escaping, no doubt – Esmeralda had been placed when condemned to the gibbet, with the colossal Palace of Justice over her head. Poor fly, that could not have stirred the smallest of its stones!

She was there, lost in the darkness, buried, entombed. Anyone who could have beheld her in this state, after having seen her laugh and dance in the sun, would have shuddered. Cold as night, cold as death, not a breath of air in her tresses, not a human sound in her ear, no longer a ray of light in her eyes, bent double, loaded with chains, crouching beside a jug and a loaf of bread upon a little straw in the pool of water formed beneath her by the damp oozing of her cell, without motion, almost without breath, she was now scarcely sensible even to suffering.

Since she had been there she neither waked nor slept. In that misery, in that dungeon, she could no more distinguish waking from sleeping, dreams from reality, than she could the day from the night. All was mingled, broken, floating, confusedly scattered in her mind. She felt nothing, knew nothing, thought nothing; at best she only dreamed. Never did living creature plunge so far into the realm of nothingness.

Thus benumbed, frozen, petrified, had she scarcely noticed the sound of a trap-door which was twice or thrice opened somewhere above her, without even admitting a ray of light, and through which a hand had thrown a crust of black bread. Yet this was her only remaining communication with mankind – the periodical visit of the jailer. One thing alone still mechanically occupied her ear; over her head the dampness filtered through the mouldy stones of the vault, and a drop of water dropped from them at regular intervals. She listened stupidly to the noise made by this drop of water as it fell into the pool beside her.

Although, indeed, she also felt, from time to time, in that sink of mire and darkness, something cold passing here and there over her foot or her arm, and she shuddered.

How long had she been there? She knew not. She had a recollection of a sentence of death pronounced somewhere against someone; then she was borne away, and she awaked icy cold in the midst of night and silence. She had crawled along upon her hands, then iron rings cut her ankles and chains clanked. She discovered that all around her was wall, that underneath her were flag-stones covered with water, and a bundle of straw; but there was neither lamp nor air-hole. Then she seated herself upon the straw, and occasionally, for a change of position, on the lowest of some stone steps in her dungeon.

At length, one day, or one night (for midnight and noon had the same hue in this sepulchre), she heard above her a louder noise than that usually made by the turnkey when he brought her bread and jug of water. She raised her head and saw a reddish light through the crevices of the sort of trap-door made in the arch of the *in pace*.

At the same time the heavy lock creaked, the trap-door grated on its rusty hinges, turned, and she beheld a lantern, a hand, and the lower part of the bodies of two men, the door being too low for her to see their heads. The light pained her so acutely that she shut her eyes.

When she reopened them the door was closed, the lantern was placed on a step of the staircase, one man alone was standing before her. A black gown fell to his feet, a cowl of the same hue concealed his face. Nothing was visible of his person, neither his face nor his hands. It looked like a long black winding-sheet standing upright, beneath which something seemed to move. She gazed fixedly for some moments at this sort of spectre.

At length the prisoner broke silence.

'Who are you?'

'A priest.'

The word, the accent, the sound of the voice made her start.

The priest continued in a hollow tone:

'Are you prepared?'

'For what?'

'To die.'

'Oh!' said she, 'will it be soon?'

'Tomorrow.'

Her head, which she had raised with a look of joy, again sank upon her bosom.

'That is very long yet,' murmured she; 'what difference would a day make to them?'

'Are you then very unhappy?' asked the priest after a short silence.

'I am very cold,' replied she.

She took her feet in her hands, a habitual gesture with unfortunate creatures who are cold, and which we have already observed in the recluse of the Tour-Roland, and her teeth chattered.

The priest's eyes appeared to be wandering from under his hood around the dungeon.

'Without light! without fire! in the water! It is horrible!'

'Yes,' answered she with the bewildered air which misery had given her. 'The day belongs to everyone; why do they give me only night?'

'Do you know,' resumed the priest, after another silence, 'why you are here?'

'I think I knew once,' said she, passing her thin fingers across her brow, as if to assist her memory, 'but I know no longer.'

All at once she began to weep like a child.

'I want to go away from here, monsieur. I am cold – I am afraid – and there are creatures that crawl over my body.'

'Well, follow me.'

So saying, the priest took her arm. The poor girl was chilled to her very vitals, yet that hand felt cold to her.

'Oh!' murmured she, ''tis the icy hand of death. Who are you?'

The priest threw back his hood; she looked: it was that sinister visage which had so long pursued her – that demon's head which had appeared to her at La Falourdel's over the adored head of her Phœbus – that eye which she last saw glaring beside a dagger.

'Hah!' she cried, pressing her hands to her eyes, with a convulsive shudder, 'it is the priest!'

'You look upon me with horror, then,' he asked at length.

Her lips contracted as if she were smiling.

'Yes,' said she; 'the executioner taunts the condemned! For months he pursues me, threatens me, terrifies me. But for him, my God, how happy I would be! It is he who has cast me into this abyss! Oh, heavens! it was he who killed – it was he who killed him – my Phœbus!'

Here she burst into sobs, and raising her eyes toward the priest:

'Oh! wretch! who are you? what have I done to you? do you then hate me so? Alas! what have you against me?'

'I love thee!' cried the priest.

Her tears suddenly ceased; she eyed him with the vacant stare of an idiot. He had fallen on his knees and was devouring her with eyes of flame.

'Dost thou hear? I love thee!' cried he again.

'What love!' ejaculated the unhappy creature.

He continued:

'The love of a damned soul!'

Both remained silent for several minutes, crushed under the weight of their emotions – he maddened, she stupefied.

'Listen,' said the priest at last, and a strange calm came over him; 'thou shalt know all. I am about to tell thee what hitherto I have scarcely dared tell myself, when I secretly questioned my conscience, in those dead hours of the night when it is so dark that it seems as though God no longer sees us. Listen. Before I saw thee, young girl, I was happy . . .'

'And I too!' sighed she feebly.

'Interrupt me not! Yes, I was happy; or, at least, I thought so. I was pure; my soul was filled with limpid light. No head was raised more proudly or more radiantly than mine. Priests consulted me on chastity, doctors on doctrines. Yes, science was all in all to me; it was a sister – and a sister sufficed me. Not but that, growing older, other ideas came across my mind. More than once my flesh was thrilled as a woman's form passed by. That force of sex and passion which, foolish youth, I had thought stifled forever, had more than once shaken convulsively the chain of the iron vows which bind me, miserable wretch, to the cold stones of the altar. But fasting, prayer, study, the macerations of the cloister again made the spirit ruler of the body. And then I shunned women. So long as the Demon sent only vague shadows of women to attack me, passing casually before my eyes, in the church, in the streets, in the fields, and scarcely recurring in my dreams, I vanquished him easily. Listen. One day . . . '

Here the priest paused, and the prisoner heard deep sighs burst from his bosom, each one seeming like the last breath of agony.

He resumed:

'One day, I was leaning on the window of my cell. I was reading. The window opened upon a square. I heard the sound of a tambourine and music. Vexed at being thus disturbed in my reverie, I glanced into the square. What I saw, others saw beside myself – and yet it was not a spectacle for mortal eye. There, in the middle of the pavement – a creature was dancing, a creature so beautiful that God would have preferred her to the Virgin – would have chosen her for His mother – would have been born of her, had she existed when He was made man. Her eyes were black and lustrous; amidst her raven hair, certain locks, through which the sunbeams shone, were glistening like threads of gold. Her feet moved so swiftly that they appeared indistinct, like the spokes of a wheel revolving rapidly. Around her head, amongst her ebon tresses, were plates of metal, which sparkled in the sun, and formed about her temples a diadem of stars. Her dress, thick-set with spangles, twinkled, blue and with a thousand sparks, like a summer night. Her brown and pliant arms twined and untwined about her waist like two silken scarfs. Her figure was of surprising beauty. Alas! young girl, it was thou! Surprised, intoxicated, charmed, I allowed myself to gaze upon thee. I looked at thee so long that suddenly I shuddered with affright. I felt that the hand of Fate was upon me.'

The priest, oppressed by emotion, again paused for a moment; then continued:

'Already half fascinated, I strove to cling to something and to stay myself from falling. I recalled the snares which Satan had already set for me. The creature before me was of that preternatural beauty which can only be of heaven or hell. That was no mere girl moulded of our common clay, and faintly lighted within by the flickering ray of a woman's spirit. It was an angel, but of darkness – of flame, not of light. At the moment that I was thinking thus, I saw beside thee a goat, a beast of the witches, which looked at me laughingly. The midday sun gilded its horns with fire. Then I perceived the snare of the Demon, and I no longer doubted that thou camest from hell, and that thou camest for my perdition. I believed it.'

Here the priest looked the prisoner in the face, and added coldly:

'I believe it still. However, the charm operated little by little. Thy dancing whirled in my brain; I felt the mysterious spell at work within me. All that should have waked in my soul was lulled to sleep; and, like those who perish in the snow, I took pleasure in yielding to that slumber.'

He made another pause and proceeded:

'Yes; from that day forth there was within me a man I knew not. I had recourse to all my remedies – the cloister, the altar, work, books – follies! Oh! how empty science sounds when we beat against it in despair a head filled with frantic passion! Knowest thou, young girl, what I saw ever after between the book and me? Thee, thy shadow, the image of the luminous apparition which had one day passed before me. But that image was no longer of the same hue; it was gloomy, funereal, darksome – like the black circle that long hangs about the vision of the imprudent one who has been gazing steadfastly at the sun.

'I sought thee. I saw thee again. Misery! When I had seen thee twice, I wished to see a thousand times, I wished to see thee always! Then – how stop short on that steep descent to hell? Then I was no longer my own master. The other end of the thread which the Demon had tied about my wings was fastened to his foot. I became vagrant and wandering like thyself, I waited for thee under porches, I spied thee out at the corners of streets, I watched thee from the top of my tower. Each night I found myself more charmed, more despairing, more fascinated, more lost!

'I had learned who thou wast – a gypsy, a Bohemian, a gitana, a zingara. How could I doubt the witchcraft? Listen. I hoped that a trial would rid me of the charm. First, I tried to have thee forbidden the square in front of Notre-Dame, hoping to forget thee if thou camest no more. Thou didst not heed. Thou camest again. Then came the idea of carrying thee off. One night I attempted it. There were two of us. Already we had laid hold on thee, when that wretched officer came upon us.

He delivered thee. Thus was he the beginning of thy misfortunes, of mine, and of his own. At length, not knowing what to do or what was to become of me, I denounced thee to the official.

'I thought I should be cured. I, also, had a confused idea that a trial would deliver thee into my hands; that in a prison I should hold thee, I should have thee; that there thou couldst not escape me; that thou hadst possessed me a sufficiently long time to give me the right to possess thee in my turn. When one does evil, one should do it thoroughly. 'Tis madness to stop midway in the monstrous! The extremity of crime has its delirium of joy. A priest and a witch may mingle in ecstasy upon the straw of a dungeon floor!

'So I denounced thee. 'Twas then that I used to terrify thee whenever I met thee. The plot which I was weaving against thee, the storm which I was brewing over thy head, burst from me in muttered threats and lightning glances. Still I hesitated. My project had its appaling sides, which made me shrink back.

'One day – again the sun was shining brightly – I beheld a man pass me who pronounced thy name and laughed, and who carried profligacy in his eyes. Damnation! I followed him. Thou knowest the rest.'

He ceased.

The young girl could find but one word:

'Oh, my Phœbus!'

'Not that name!' said the priest, seizing her arm with violence. 'Pronounce not that name! Oh! Unhappy wretches that we are; 'tis that name which has ruined us! or rather, we have ruined each other by the inexplicable play of fate! Thou art suffering, art thou not? Thou art cold; darkness blinds thee; the dungeon wraps thee round; but, perhaps, thou has still some light shining within thee – were it only thy childish love for that empty being who was trifling with thy heart? while I – bear the dungeon within me; within me is winter, ice, despair; I have the darkness in my soul.

'Knowest thou all that I have suffered? I was present at thy trial. I was seated on the bench with the officials. Yes, under one of those priestly hoods were the contortions of a damned spirit. When thou wast brought in, I was there; when thou wast interrogated, I was there. The den of wolves! 'Twas my own crime; 'twas my own gibbet they were slowly constructing over thy head! At each deposition, at each proof, at each pleading, I was there; I could count each of thy steps on the road of agony. I was there, again, when that wild beast . . . Oh! I had not foreseen the torture! Listen. I followed thee to the chamber of anguish. I saw thee stripped and handled by the vile hands of the torturer. I saw thy foot – that foot, upon which I would have given an empire to press a single kiss and die; that foot, beneath which I would with rapture have been crushed – that foot I beheld encased in the horrible boot, that boot which converts the limb of a living being into bleeding pulp! Oh! wretched me! while I looked on at that I grasped beneath my sackcloth a dagger with which I lacerated my breast. At the shriek which thou utteredst, I plunged it in my flesh; at a second cry, it would have entered my heart. Look; I think it still bleeds.'

He opened his cassock. His breast was indeed torn as if by a tiger's claws, and in his side was a large, ill-closed wound.

The prisoner shrank back with horror.

'Oh!' said the priest, 'girl, have pity on me! Thou thinkest thyself unhappy. Alas! alas! thou knowest not what misery is. Oh! to love a woman – to be a priest – to be hated – to love her with all the fury of your soul – to feel that you would give for the least of her smiles your blood, your vitals, your reputation, your salvation, immortality and eternity, this life and the other – to regret you are not a king, a genius, an emperor, an archangel, God, that you might place a greater slave beneath her feet – to clasp her day and night in your dreams, in your thoughts; and to see her in love with the trappings of a soldier, and have nothing to offer her but a priest's dirty cassock, which will terrify and disgust her. To be present with your jealousy and your rage while she lavishes on a miserable, blustering imbecile treasures of love and beauty! To behold that body whose form inflames you, that bosom which has so much sweetness, that flesh tremble and blush under the kisses of another! Oh heavens! to love her foot, her arm, her shoulder! to think of her blue veins, of her brown skin, until one writhes for nights together on the pavement of one's cell; and to see all those caresses one has dreamed of end in torture! to have succeeded only in laying her on the bed of leather! Oh, these are the true pincers heated at the fires of hell!'

The priest writhed on the wet pavement and beat his head against the edges of the stone steps. The young girl listened to him, looked at him.

When he ceased speaking, panting and exhausted, she repeated in an undertone:

'Oh, my Phœbus!'

The priest dragged himself towards her on his knees.

'I implore thee,' cried he, 'if thou has any bowels of compassion, repulse me not! Oh! I love thee! I am a miserable wretch! When thou utterest that name, unhappy girl, it is as if

thou wert grinding between thy teeth every fibre of my heart!
. . . Oh! how happy could we be! We would flee; I would help
thee to flee; we would go somewhere; we would seek that spot on
the earth where the sun is brightest, the trees most luxuriant, the
sky the bluest. We would love each other; we would pour our two
souls one into the other and we would each have an inextinguishable thirst for the other which we would quench incessantly
and together at the inexhaustible fountain of love!'

She interrupted him with a loud and terrible laugh.

'Look, father! you have blood upon your fingers!'

The priest remained for some moments petrified, his eyes fixed
on his hand.

'Yes, 'tis well,' he resumed at length with strange gentleness;
'insult me, taunt me, overwhelm me with scorn! but come, come
away. Let us hasten. It is to be tomorrow, I tell thee. The gibbet
on the Grève, thou knowest! It is ever ready. 'Tis horrible! to
see thee borne in that tumbrel! Tomorrow! tomorrow! the
gibbet! thy execution! Oh! save thyself! spare me!'

He seized her arm; he was frantic; he strove to drag her
away.

She fixed her eye intently on him.

'What has become of my Phœbus?'

'Ah!' said the priest, letting go her arm, 'you have no pity!'

'What has become of Phœbus?' she repeated coldly.

'He is dead!' cried the priest.

'Dead!' said she, still cold and passionless; 'then why do you
talk to me of living?'

He heard her not.

'Oh, yes!' said he, as if talking to himself, 'he must indeed
be dead. The blade entered deep. I believe I touched his heart
with the point. Oh! my very soul was in that dagger's point!'

The young girl rushed upon him like an enraged tigress, and
thrust him against the flight of steps with supernatural strength.

'Begone, monster! begone, murderer! leave me to die! May
the blood of us both mark thy brow with an everlasting stain! . . .
Be thine! priest? Never! never! nothing shall unite us! not hell
itself! Begone, accursed! Never!'

The priest had stumbled to the steps. He silently disengaged
his feet from the folds of his cassock, took up his lantern, and
began slowly to ascend the steps leading to the door; he reopened
the door and went out.

All at once the young girl beheld his head re-appear; his face
wore a frightful expression, and he cried to her, hoarse with rage
and despair:

'I tell thee, he is dead!'

She fell face downwards on the ground, and no sound was heard in the dungeon save the sob of the drop of water which made the pool palpitate amid the darkness.

5

Phœbus, however, was not dead. Men of that stamp are hard to kill. When Maître Philippe Lheulier, king's advocate extraordinary, had said to poor Esmeralda, 'he is dying,' it was an error or in jest. When the archdeacon had repeated to the condemned girl, 'he is dead,' the fact was that he knew nothing about the matter, but he believed it, he made sure of it and he had no doubt of it. It would have been too hard for him to give favorable news of his rival to the woman he loved. Any man would have done the same in his place.

Not that Phœbus's wound was not severe, but it was less so than the archdeacon flattered himself. The surgeon, to whose house the soldiers of the watch had at once carried him, had, for a week, feared for his life, and had even told him so in Latin. However, youth triumphed; and as often happens, notwithstanding prognostics and diagnostics, Nature amused herself by saving the patient, in spite of the physician. It was while he was still lying upon the leech's pallet that he underwent the first interrogatories of Philippe Lheulier and the official inquisitors, which he had found especially wearisome. Accordingly, one fine morning, feeling himself better, he had left his golden spurs in payment to the man of medicine, and taken himself off. This, however, had not in the least affected the judicial proceedings. Justice in those days cared little about clearness and precision in the proceedings against a criminal. Provided only that the accused was hung, that was all that was necessary. Now the judges had ample proof against La Esmeralda. They believed Phœbus to be dead – and that was the end of the matter.

Phœbus, for his part, had fled to no great distance. He had simply rejoined his company in garrison at Queue-en-Brie, in the Isle of France, a few stages from Paris.

After all, it did not please him in the least to appear in this suit. He had a vague impression that he would play a ridiculous part in it. In fact, he did not very well know what to think of the whole affair. Irreligious and superstitious, like every soldier who is nothing but a soldier, when he came to question himself about this adventure, he was not altogether without his suspicions of the little goat, of the singular fashion in which he had first met La Esmeralda, of the no less strange manner in which she had betrayed her love, of her being a gypsy, and lastly of the spectre monk. He perceived in all these incidents much more magic than love; probably a sorceress; perhaps a devil.

Phœbus, therefore, soon set his mind at rest in regard to the enchantress Esmeralda or Similar, as he called her, to the dagger thrust which he had received from the gypsy-girl, or from the spectre monk (it mattered little to him which), and to the issue of the trial. But no sooner was his heart vacant on that score, than the image of Fleur-de-Lys returned thither; for the heart of Captain Phœbus, like the natural philosophy of the day, abhorred a vacuum.

Fleur-de-Lys was his last flame but one – a pretty girl, a delightful dowry. Accordingly, one fine morning, quite cured, and fairly presuming that after two months had elapsed, the affair of the gypsy-girl must be over and forgotten, the amorous cavalier arrived on a prancing horse at the door of the Gondelaurier mansion.

Fleur-de-Lys had still weighing upon her heart the scene of the sorceress with her goat and its accursed alphabet, and the lengthened absence of Phœbus. Nevertheless, when she beheld her captain enter, she thought him so handsome, his doublet so new, his baldrick so shining, and his air so impassioned, that she blushed with pleasure.

The young lady was seated near the window, still embroidering her grotto of Neptunus. The captain was leaning over the back of the chair, while she murmured to him her gentle upbraidings.

'What have you been doing with yourself for these two months past, you naughty man?'

'I swear,' replied Phœbus, a little embarrassed by the question, 'that you are beautiful enough to set an archbishop to dreaming.'

She could not help smiling.

'Good, good, sir. Let my beauty alone and answer me. Fine beauty, indeed!'

'Well, my dear cousin, I was recalled to the garrison.'

'But that is quite close by, sir. How happened it that you came not once to see me?'

Here Phœbus was very seriously perplexed. 'Because – the service – and then, charming cousin, I have been ill.'

'Ill!' she repeated in alarm.

'Yes – wounded.'

'Wounded!'

The poor girl was quite overcome.

'Oh, do not be frightened at that,' said Phœbus, carelessly; 'it was nothing. A quarrel! – a sword cut – what is that to you?'

The mendacious captain was well aware that an affair of honor always set a man off to advantage in the eyes of a woman. In fact, Fleur-de-Lys looked him in the face with mingled sensations of fear, pleasure and admiration. Still, she was not completely reassured.

'Provided that you are wholly cured, my Phœbus!' said she. 'And whence arose this quarrel?'

'Oh, I know not; a mere nothing; a horse; a remark! Fair cousin,' he exclaimed, by way of turning the conversation, 'what noise is that in the square?' He went to the window.

'I do not know,' said Fleur-de-Lys; 'it appears that a witch is to do penance this morning before the church, and thereafter to be hanged.'

Phœbus returned to lean over the back of the chair of his betrothed; a charming situation, whence his libertine gaze could invade every opening in Fleur-de-Lys's collarette. This collarette gaped so opportunely, and revealed to him so many exquisite things, and led him to divine so many others, that Phœbus, dazzled by this skin with its gleam of satin, said to himself, 'How can one love any but a fair skin?'

Both were silent. The young girl raised sweet, enraptured eyes to him, from time to time, and their hair mingled in a ray of spring sunshine.

'Phœbus,' said Fleur-de-Lys suddenly, in a low tone, 'we are to be married in three months – swear to me that you have never loved any woman but myself.'

'I swear it, fair angel!' replied Phœbus; and his passionate gaze combined with the truthful tone of his voice to convince Fleur-de-Lys. Perhaps, indeed, at that moment, he himself believed what he was saying.

Meanwhile, the good mother, delighted to see the betrothed pair on such excellent terms, had left the apartment to attend to some household matter. Phœbus observed it; and this so much emboldened the adventurous captain, that some very strange ideas entered his brain. Fleur-de-Lys loved him; he was her betrothed; she was alone with him; his former inclination for her had revived, not with all its freshness, but with all its ardor; after all, there was no great harm in tasting one's fruit before it is harvested. Fleur-de-Lys was suddenly alarmed at the expression of his glance.

'Good heavens!' said she, flushed and uneasy, 'I am very warm!'

'I think, indeed,' returned Phœbus, 'it must be almost noon. The sun is troublesome; we need only draw the curtains.'

'No, no!' cried the trembling damsel; 'on the contrary, I need air.'

And, like a fawn that scents the breath of the approaching pack, she rose, hurried to the window, opened it, and rushed upon the balcony.

Phœbus, considerably vexed, followed her.

The Place du Parvis Notre-Dame, upon which, as we know, the balcony looked, presented, at that moment, a singular and sinister spectacle.

'Oh, heavens!' said Fleur-de-Lys, 'the poor creature!'

This thought filled with sadness the glance which she cast upon the crowd. The captain, much more occupied with her than with that pack of rabble, was amorously fingering her girdle behind. She turned around with smiling entreaty.

'For pity's sake, let me alone, Phœbus! if my mother were to return she would see your hand.'

At that moment, the clock of Notre-Dame slowly struck twelve. A murmur of satisfaction burst from the crowd. The last vibration of the twelfth stroke had hardly died away, when all the heads surged like the waves before a sudden gale, and an immense shout went up from the pavement, from the windows, and from the roofs, 'There she is!'

A tumbrel drawn by a strong Norman dray horse, and quite surrounded by horsemen in violet livery with white crosses, had just entered the square from the Rue Saint-Pierre-aux-Bœufs. The sergeants of the watch cleared a passage for it through the crowd by a vigorous use of their whiteleather whips.

In the fatal cart sat a young girl, her hands tied behind her, and with no priest at her side. She was in her shift; her long black hair (the custom then was to cut it only at the foot of the gibbet) fell in disorder upon her half-bared throat and shoulders. Athwart that waving hair, more glossy than a raven's plumage, a rough, gray cord was seen, twisted and knotted, chafing her delicate skin and winding about the poor girl's graceful neck like an earthworm around a flower. Beneath that rope glittered a small amulet, ornamented with bits of green glass, which had been left to her, no doubt, because nothing is refused to those about to die. The spectators at the windows could see in the bottom of the tumbrel her naked legs, which she strove to conceal under her as by a final feminine instinct. At her feet lay a little goat, bound. The prisoner was holding together with her teeth her ill-tied chemise. It seemed as if even in her misery she still suffered from being thus exposed almost naked before all eyes. Alas! it was not for such shocks that modesty was made.

'Jesus!' said Fleur-de-Lys hastily to the captain, 'look there, fair cousin – it is that horrid gypsy-girl with the goat.'

119

So saying, she turned to Phœbus. His eyes were fixed on the tumbrel. He was very pale.

'What gypsy-girl with the goat?' he stammered.

'Why,' rejoined Fleur-de-Lys, 'do you not remember?'

Phœbus interrupted her:

'I do not know what you mean.'

He stepped back to re-enter the room, but Fleur-de-Lys, whose jealousy, already so deeply stirred by this same gypsy-girl, was now re-awakened, cast at him a glance full of penetration and mistrust. She now vaguely recollected having heard a captain mentioned who had been implicated in the trial of this sorceress.

'What ails you?' said she to Phœbus; 'one would think that this woman disturbed you.'

Phœbus forced a sneering smile.

'Me! not the least in the world! Me, indeed!'

'Remain, then,' returned she imperiously, 'and let us see the end.'

Before the central doorway of the church the cart stopped. The escort drew up in line on either side. The mob was silenced; and amid this silence so solemn and anxious the two halves of the great door turned, as if of themselves, upon their hinges, which creaked like the sound of a fife. Then the deep interior of the church was seen in its whole extent, gloomy, hung with black, faintly lighted by a few wax tapers twinkling afar off upon the high altar, yawning like the mouth of a cavern upon the square resplendent with sunshine. At the farthest extremity in the dusk of the chancel, was dimly seen a colossal silver cross, standing out in relief against a black cloth, which hung from the roof to the pavement. The whole nave was deserted; but heads of priests were seen moving confusedly in the distant choir stalls; and at the moment when the great door opened there burst from the church a loud, solemn and monotonous chant, hurling as it were in gusts, fragments of doleful psalms at the head of the condemned one.

The people listened devoutly.

The unfortunate girl, bewildered, seemed to lose her sight and her consciousness in the dark interior of the church. Her pale lips moved as if in prayer; and when the hangman's assistant approached to help her down from the cart, he heard her repeating in a whisper, this word: 'Phœbus.'

They untied her hands, made her alight, accompanied by her goat, which was also unbound, and which bleated with joy at finding itself free. She was then led barefoot over the hard pavement to the foot of the steps leading to the portal. The cord about her neck trailed behind her like a serpent pursuing her.

Then the chanting in the church ceased. A great golden cross and a row of wax candles began to move through the gloom. The halberds of the motley-dressed beadles clanked, and a few moments later a long procession of priests in chasubles and deacons in dalmatics marched solemnly toward the prisoner, singing psalms as they came into view. But her eyes were riveted upon him who walked at their head, immediately after the cross-bearer.

'Oh!' she said in a low tone with a shudder, ''tis he again! the priest!'

When he appeared in the broad daylight, beneath the lofty arched portal, covered with an ample cope of silver, barred with a black cross, he was so pale that more than one amongst the crowd thought that one of the marble bishops kneeling upon the monuments in the choir had risen and had come forth to receive on the threshold of the tomb her who was about to die.

She, equally pale and rigid, hardly noticed that they had placed in her hand a heavy lighted taper of yellow wax. She had not heard the shrill voice of the clerk, reading the fatal lines of the penance; only, when told to answer amen, she said 'Amen!' It was only the sight of the priest making a sign to her guards to retire, and himself advancing toward her, that brought back to her any sense of life and strength.

The archdeacon approached her slowly. Even in this extremity she saw him gaze upon her nakedness with eyes glittering with passion, jealousy and desire. Then he said to her in a loud voice, 'Young woman, have you asked pardon of God for your sins and your offences?' He bent to her ear, and added (the spectators supposed that he was receiving her last confession), 'Wilt thou be mine? I can even yet save thee!'

She looked steadily at him: 'Begone, demon! or I denounce thee!'

He smiled – a horrible smile. 'They will not believe thee. Thou wilt but add scandal to guilt. Answer quickly! wilt thou be mine?'

'What hast thou done with my Phœbus?'

'He is dead,' said the priest.

At this moment the miserable archdeacon raised his head mechanically, and saw, at the opposite side of the square, on the balcony of the Gondelaurier house, the captain standing by Fleur-de-Lys. He staggered, passed his hand over his eyes, looked again, muttered a malediction, and all his features were violently contorted.

'Well, then, die, thou!' said he, between his teeth; 'no one shall have thee!'

Then raising his hand over the gypsy, he exclaimed, in a

sepulchral voice, '*I nunc anima anceps, et sit tibi Deus misericors.*' (Go thy way now, lingering soul, and may God have mercy upon thee!)

He turned his back upon the prisoner; his head again fell upon his breast; his hands were crossed; he rejoined his train of priests, and a moment later he disappeared with cross, candles and copes beneath the dim arches of the cathedral, and his sonorous voice gradually died away.

The unhappy creature at the moment of re-mounting the fatal cart, and setting out on her last stage, was perhaps seized with some poignant clinging to life. She raised her dry, red eyes to heaven, to the sun, to the silvery clouds, intermingled with patches of brilliant blue; then she cast them around her upon the ground, the people, the houses. All at once, while the man in yellow was pinioning her arms, she uttered a terrible cry, a cry of joy. Yonder, on that balcony, at the corner of the Place, she had just caught sight of him, her friend, her lord, Phœbus, the other apparition of her life!

The judge had lied! the priest had lied! it was he indeed, she could not doubt it. He was there, handsome, alive, dressed in his brilliant uniform, his plume on his head, his sword by his side!

'Phœbus!' she cried, 'my Phœbus!'

Then she saw the captain knit his brows; a fine young woman, leaning upon his arm, looked at him with scornful lip and angry eye; then Phœbus uttered some words which did not reach her; and then he and the lady both disappeared precipitately through the window of the balcony, which closed after them.

'Phœbus!' she cried, wildly; 'dost thou too believe it?'

A monstrous thought had dawned upon her. She recollected that she had been condemned for the murder of Phœbus de Chateaupers.

She had borne up until now, but this last blow was too severe. She fell senseless upon the ground.

'Come,' said Charmolue, 'carry her to the cart, and make an end of it.'

No one had observed in the gallery of statues of the kings, carved just above the arches of the portal, a strange-looking spectator, who, until now, watched all that passed with such impassiveness, a neck so out-stretched, a visage so deformed, that, but for his parti-colored red and violet garb, he might have been taken for one of the stone monsters through whose jaws the long gutters of the cathedral have disgorged themselves for six centuries past. This spectator had missed nothing that had taken place since midday in front of the portal of Notre-Dame. And at the very beginning, without anyone noticing him, he had securely fastened to one of the small columns of the gallery a strong knotted rope, the other end of which trailed on the top of the steps below. This done, he began to look on tranquilly, whistling from time to time when a blackbird flitted past.

Suddenly, at the moment when the executioner's assistants were preparing to execute Charmolue's phlegmatic order, he threw his leg over the balustrade of the gallery, gripped the rope with his feet, his knees and his hands; then he was seen to slide down the façade, as a drop of rain slips down a window-pane, run up to the two sub-executioners with the speed of a cat just dropped from a house-top, knock them down with two enormous fists, pick up the gypsy with one hand, as a child might a doll, and leap, at one bound, into the church, lifting the girl above his head, and shouting in a tremendous voice, 'Sanctuary!'

This was done with such rapidity that, had it been night, the whole might have been seen by the glare of a single flash of lightning.

'Sanctuary! Sanctuary!' repeated the crowd; and the clapping of ten thousand hands made Quasimodo's only eye sparkle with joy and pride.

This shock restored the prisoner to her senses. She raised her eyelids, looked at Quasimodo, then closed them again suddenly, as if terrified at her deliverer.

Charmolue, the executioners and the whole escort were confounded. In fact, within the precincts of Notre-Dame the condemned was inviolable. The cathedral was a recognized place of refuge; all temporal jurisdiction expired upon its threshold.

Quasimodo had stopped under the great portal. His broad feet seemed to rest as solidly upon the floor of the church as the heavy Roman pillars themselves. His big bushy head was buried between his shoulders like the head of a lion, which also has a mane, but no neck. He held the trembling girl, suspended in his horny hands, like a piece of white drapery, but he carried her with as much care as if he feared he should break or injure her. He seemed to feel that a thing so delicate, exquisite and precious was not made for such hands as his. At times he looked as if he dared not touch her, even with his breath. Then, all at once, he would press her close in his arms to his angular breast, as his own, his treasure, as her mother might have done. His gnome-like eye, resting upon her, flooded her with tenderness, grief and pity, and was suddenly lifted, flashing fire. Then the women laughed and wept, the crowd stamped their feet with enthusiasm, for at that moment Quasimodo had a beauty of his own. He was fine; he, that orphan, that foundling, that outcast; he felt himself august and strong.

However, after a few moments of triumph, Quasimodo plunged abruptly into the church with his burden. The people, fond of any display of prowess, sought him with their eyes under the gloomy nave, regretting that he had so quickly withdrawn from their acclamations. All at once he was seen to reappear at one extremity of the gallery of the kings of France. He ran along it like a madman, holding his conquest aloft, and shouting: 'Sanctuary!' Fresh plaudits burst from the multitude. Having traversed the gallery, he plunged again into the interior of the church. A moment later he reappeared upon the upper platform, with the gypsy still in his arms, still running wildly along, still shouting 'Sanctuary!' and the throng applauded. Finally he made a third appearance on the top of the tower of the great bell: from thence he seemed to show exultingly to the whole city her whom he had saved; and his thundering voice, that voice so rarely heard by anyone, and never by himself, thrice repeated with frenzy that pierced the very clouds: 'Sanctuary! Sanctuary! Sanctuary!'

BOOK SEVEN

1

Claude Frollo was no longer in Notre-Dame when his adopted son thus abruptly cut the fatal knot in which the unhappy archdeacon had bound the gypsy-girl and caught himself. On returning into the sacristy, he had torn off the albe, cope and stole; flung them all into the hands of the amazed verger; fled through the private door of the cloister; ordered a boatman of the Terrain to carry him over to the left bank of the Seine, and plunged in among the hilly streets of the University, going he knew not whither; meeting, at every step, parties of men and women hastening gaily towards the Pont Saint Michel, in the hope that they might still 'arrive in time' to see the witch hanged.

He skirted Mount Sainte Geneviève, and finally emerged from the town by the Porte Saint Victor. He continued his flight so long as he could see, on turning, the towered enclosure of the University, and the scattered houses of the faubourg; but when at last a ridge completely hid that odious Paris he paused, and it seemed to him as if he breathed more freely.

Then frightful ideas rushed upon his mind. He saw once more clear into his soul, and shuddered. He thought of that unfortunate girl who had destroyed him, and whom he had destroyed. He cast a haggard eye over the two winding paths, along which fate had driven their separate destinies, to that point of intersection at which she had pitilessly dashed them against each other. He thought of the folly of eternal vows, the emptiness of chastity, science, religion, virtue, the uselessness of God. He indulged in evil thought to his heart's content, and, while plunging deeper into them, he felt as if the fiend were laughing within him.

And then he laughed anew, as he reflected that Phœbus was alive; that, after all, the captain lived, was light-hearted and happy, had finer doublets than ever, and a new mistress, whom he brought to see the old one hanged. And he sneered at himself with redoubled bitterness, when he reflected that, of all the living beings whose death he had desired, the only creature he did not hate, was the only one who had not escaped him.

Then his thoughts wandered from the captain to the populace,

125

and he was overcome with jealousy of an unheard of kind. He reflected that the people, also, the entire mob, had had before their eyes the woman he loved, in her shift, almost naked. He wrung his hands in agony at the thought that the woman, whose form half seen by him alone in darkness, would have afforded him supreme delight, had been exposed, in broad daylight, at noontide, to the gaze of a whole multitude, clad as for a bridal night.

Oh, she – still she! It was this fixed idea that haunted him incessantly, that tortured him, that turned his brain and gnawed his vitals. He regretted nothing, repented nothing; all that he had done, he was ready to do again; he liked better to see her in the hands of the executioner than in the arms of the captain. But he suffered; suffered so intensely, that at moments he tore out his hair by handfuls to see if it were not turning white.

Thus he sped through the country until nightfall. This flight from Nature, life, himself, man, God, everything, lasted the whole day. Sometimes he threw himself face downward upon the earth, and tore up the young corn with his nails. Sometimes he paused in some deserted village street, and his thoughts were so unendurable that he would seize his head in both hands, as if to tear it from his shoulders and dash it on the stones.

Toward the hour of sunset he examined himself again, and found himself almost mad. The storm which had been raging within him from the moment when he had lost all hope and wish to save the gypsy, had left him unconscious of a single sound idea, a single rational thought. His reason lay prostrate, almost utterly destroyed. His mind retained but two distinct images, La Esmeralda and the gibbet, all the rest was black.

It is remarkable that, during all this torture, he never seriously thought of putting an end to himself. The wretch was made thus; he clung to life – perhaps, indeed, he really saw hell in prospect.

When he once more entered the streets of Paris, the people passing to and fro in the light of the shop-windows appeared to him like an everlasting coming and going of spectres about him. There were strange noises in his ears; extraordinary fancies disturbed his brain. He saw neither houses, nor pavement, nor vehicles, nor men and women, but a chaos of undefined objects blending one into another.

Eventually the archdeacon reached Notre-Dame, whose enormous towers he could see rising in the dark above the houses.

When he arrived, panting, at the Place du Parvis, he shrunk back, and dared not lift his eyes toward the fatal edifice.

'Oh,' he murmured to himself, 'is it possible that such a thing took place here today, this very morning!'

However, he ventured to glance at the church. The front was dark, the sky beyond it glittered with stars, the crescent moon, in her flight upward from the horizon, at that moment reached the summit of the right hand tower, and seemed to have perched upon it, like a luminous bird, on the edge of the black trifoliated balustrade.

The cloister door was closed; but the archdeacon always carried about him the key of the tower, in which was his laboratory; availing himself of it he entered the church.

He found within it the gloom and silence of a cave. By the heavy shadows falling on all sides in broad masses, he knew that the hangings put up for the morning's ceremony had not been removed. The great silver cross shone from the depths of the gloom, dotted with glittering points, like the milky way of that sepulchral night. The long windows of the choir showed the tops of their pointed arches above the black drapery, their stained glass panes admitting a faint ray of moonlight, had only the doubtful colors of the night, a sort of violet, white and blue, of a tint to be found nowhere else but on the faces of the dead.

He fled across the church. Then it seemed to him as if the church itself took life and motion – that each of the great columns was turning into an enormous paw that beat the ground with its big stone spatula, and that the gigantic cathedral was a sort of prodigious elephant, breathing and marching, with its pillars for legs, its two towers for tusks, and the immense black cloth for its housings.

He had one moment of relief. As he plunged into the side aisles, he perceived a reddish light behind a group of pillars. He rushed towards it as to a star. It was the feeble lamp which burned day and night above the public breviary of Notre-Dame beneath its iron grating. He cast his eye eagerly upon the sacred book, in the hope of finding there some sentence of consolation or encouragement. The volume was open at this passage of Job, over which he ran his burning eye:

'And a spirit passed before my face; and I heard a small voice; and the hair of my flesh stood up.'

On reading this dismal sentence, he felt as a blind man would whose fingers are pricked by the staff which he has picked up. His knees failed him, and he sank upon the pavement, thinking of her who had that day suffered death.

He must have remained long in this posture – neither thinking, nor feeling, helpless and passive, in the hands of the demon. At length some strength returned to him; it occurred to him to take refuge in the tower, near his faithful Quasimodo. He rose; and, as fear was upon him, he took the lamp of the breviary to light him. This was a sacrilege; but he had ceased to heed such trifles.

He slowly climbed the stairs of the towers, filled with a secret dread, which must have been shared by the few passers-by in the square, who saw the mysterious light of his lamp moving at that late hour from loophole to loophole, to the top of the tower.

All at once he felt a breath of cool air on his face, and found himself under the doorway of the upper gallery. The night was cold; the sky was streaked with hurrying clouds, whose large, white masses drifted one upon another like river ice breaking up after a frost. The crescent moon, stranded in the midst of them, looked like a celestial vessel caught among those icebergs of the air.

He lowered his gaze and contemplated for a moment through the railing of slender columns which unites the towers, afar off, through a light veil of mist and smoke, the silent throng of the roofs of Paris, steep, innumerable, crowded and small as the ripples of a calm sea on a summer night.

The moon gave but a feeble light, which imparted to earth and sky an ashy hue.

At this moment the Cathedral clock raised its shrill, cracked voice. Midnight rang out. The priest thought of mid-day. Twelve o'clock had come again.

'Oh,' he whispered to himself, 'she must be cold by this time.'

Suddenly a puff of wind extinguished his lamp, and almost at the same instant there appeared, at the opposite corner of the tower, a shade, a something white, a shape, a female form. He started. By the side of this female form was that of a little goat, that mingled its bleat with the last sound of the bell.

He had strength enough to look – it was she!

She was pale, she was sad. Her hair fell over her shoulders as in the morning, but there was no rope about her neck, her hands were no longer bound; she was free, she was dead.

She was clad in white, and over her head was thrown a white veil.

She came toward him slowly, looking up to heaven. The unearthly goat followed her. He felt as if turned to stone, and too heavy to escape. At each step that she advanced he took one backwards, and that was all. In this way he retreated beneath the dark arch of the stairway. He froze at the thought that she might perhaps enter there too; had she done so, he would have died of terror.

She did, in fact, approach the staircase door, paused there for some moments, looked steadily into the darkness, without appearing to perceive the priest, and passed on. He thought she looked taller than when she was alive. He saw the moon through her white robes; he heard her breathe.

When she had passed on, he began to descend the stairs as slowly as he had seen the spectre move, imagining himself a spectre also – haggard, his hair erect, his extinguished lamp still in his hand – and, as he descended the spiral stairs, he distinctly heard in his ear a mocking voice repeating: 'And a spirit passed before my face; and I heard a small voice; and the hair of my flesh stood up.'

2

Every town in the Middle Ages, and up to the time of Louis XII, every town in France had its places of refuge, or sanctuaries. These sanctuaries, amid the deluge of penal laws and barbarous jurisdictions that inundated the state, were like so many islands rising above the level of human justice. Any criminal that landed upon them was saved.

At Notre-Dame it was a tiny chamber, situated on the roof of the side aisle beneath the flying buttresses. Here it was that, after his wild and triumphal race along the towers and galleries, Quasimodo deposited La Esmeralda. So long as that race lasted, the damsel had not recovered her senses, half stupefied, half awake, having only a vague perception that she was ascending in the air, that she was floating, flying there, that something was carrying her upward from the earth. From time to time she heard the loud laugh and the harsh voice of Quasimodo at her ear. She half-opened her eyes; then beneath her she saw, confusedly, Paris, all checkered with its countless roofs of tile and slate, like a red and blue mosaic, and above her head Quasimodo's frightful but joy-illumined face. Her eyelids fell; she believed that all was over, that she had been executed during her swoon, and that the misshapen spirit which had presided over her destiny had laid hold of her and was bearing her away. She dared not look at him, but surrendered herself to fate.

But when the breathless and disheveled bell-ringer laid her down in the cell of refuge; when she felt his clumsy hands gently untying the cord that had cut into her arms, she experienced that kind of shock which startles out of their sleep those on board a ship that runs aground in the middle of a dark night. Her ideas awoke also, and returned to her one by one. She saw that she was in Notre-Dame; she remembered having been snatched from the hands of the executioner; that Phœbus was living; that Phœbus loved her no longer; and these two ideas, one of which imparted so much bitterness to the other, presenting themselves at once to the poor girl, she turned to

Quasimodo, who remained standing before her, and whose aspect frightened her, and said to him: 'Why did you save me?'

He looked anxiously at her, as if striving to guess what she said. She repeated her question. He then gave her another look of profound sadness, and fled.

She was amazed.

A few moments later he returned, bringing a bundle, which he had laid at her feet. It contained apparel which certain charitable women had left for her at the threshold of the church.

Then she looked down at herself, saw that she was almost naked, and blushed. Life had returned.

Quasimodo seemed to participate in this feeling of modesty. Covering his eye with his broad hand, he again departed, but with lingering steps.

She hastily dressed herself. It was a white robe with a white veil, the habit of a novice of the Hôtel-Dieu.

She had scarcely finished before Quasimodo returned. He carried a basket under one arm and a mattress under the other. This basket contained a bottle, bread and some other provisions. He set the basket on the ground, and said, 'Eat.' He spread out the mattress on the flag-stones, and said, 'Sleep.'

It was his own meal, his own bed, that the bell-ringer had brought her.

The Egyptian lifted her eyes to his face to thank him, but could not utter a word. The poor fellow was absolutely hideous. She drooped her head with a thrill of horror.

Then he said to her:

'I frightened you. I am very ugly, am I not? Do not look at me, only listen to me. In the daytime you will stay here; at night you can walk about all over the church. But stir not a step out of it, either by night or by day. You would be lost. They would kill you, and I should die.'

Moved by his words, she raised her head to reply, but he was gone. Alone once more, she pondered on the singular words of this almost monstrous being, and struck by the tone of his voice, so hoarse and yet so gentle.

When evening came she thought the night so beautiful, the moonlight so soft, that she made the circuit of the gallery which surrounds the church. It afforded her some relief, so calm did the earth appear when viewed from that height.

3

On the following morning she perceived, on awaking, that she had slept. This strange fact amazed her; she had been so long unaccustomed to sleep! A bright beam from the rising sun came in at her window, and shone in on her face. But with the sun, she saw at the window an object that frightened her – the unfortunate face of Quasimodo. She involuntarily closed her eyes again, but in vain; she fancied that she still saw, through her rosy lids, that gnome's mask, one-eyed and gap-toothed. Then, still keeping her eyes shut, she heard a rough voice saying, very gently:

'Do not be afraid. I am your friend. I came to watch you sleep. It does not hurt you, does it, that I should come and see you sleep? What does it matter to you if I am here when you have your eyes shut? Now I am going. Stay, I have placed myself behind the wall; now you may open your eyes again.'

There was something still more plaintive than these words; it was the tone in which they were uttered. The gypsy, touched by it, opened her eyes. He was no longer at the window. She went to it and saw the poor hunchback crouching in a corner of the wall, in a sad and resigned attitude. She made an effort to overcome the repugnance with which he inspired her. 'Come hither,' she said to him, gently. From the motion of her lips Quasimodo thought she was bidding him to go away; the he rose up and retreated, limping, slowly, with drooping head, not venturing to raise to the young girl his face full of despair. 'Come hither, I say,' cried she; but he continued to move off. Then she darted out of the cell, ran to him, and took hold of his arm. On feeling her touch, Quasimodo trembled in every limb. He lifted a beseeching eye; and finding that she was trying to draw him with her, his whole face beamed with joy and tenderness. She tried to make him enter her cell; but he persisted in remaining on the threshold. 'No, no,' said he, 'the owl enters not the nest of the lark.'

Then she threw herself gracefully upon her couch, with her goat asleep at her feet. Both were motionless for several minutes, contemplating in silence – he, so much grace – she, so much ugliness. Every moment she discovered in Quasimodo some additional deformity. Her eye wandered from his crooked legs to the hump on his back, from the hump on his back to his one eye. She could not understand how a being so awkwardly fashioned could be in existence. But withal there was so much sadness and gentleness about him that she began to be reconciled to it.

He was the first to break silence. 'So you were telling me to return.'

She nodded affirmatively, and said, 'Yes.'

He understood the motion of her head. 'Alas!' said he, as though hesitating whether to finish, 'I am – I am deaf.'

131

'Poor man!' exclaimed the gypsy-girl, with an expression of kindly pity.

He smiled sorrowfully.

'You think that was all I lacked, do you not? Yes, I am deaf. That is the way I am made. It is horrible, is it not? And you — you are beautiful.'

There was so deep a sense of his wretchedness in the poor creature's tone, that she had not the courage to say a word. Besides, he would not have heard it. He continued:

'Never did I see my ugliness as now. When I compare myself with you, I do indeed pity myself, poor unhappy monster that I am. I must look to you like a beast, eh? You — you are a sunbeam, a dewdrop, a bird's song. As for me — I am something frightful, neither man nor beast — something harder, and more trodden under foot, and more unshapely than a flint-stone.'

Then he began to laugh, and that laugh was the most heartbreaking thing in the world. He went on:

'Yes, I am deaf, but you will speak to me by gestures, by signs. I have a master who talks to me that way. And then, I shall, very soon, know your wish from the movement of your lips, and from your look.'

'Well then,' replied she, smiling, 'tell me why you saved me.'

He watched her attentively as she spoke.

'I understand,' he answered, 'you ask me why I saved you. You have forgotten a poor wretch that tried to carry you off one night — a poor wretch to whom you brought relief, the very next day, on their infamous pillory; a drop of water and a little pity. That is more than I can repay with my life. You have forgotten that poor wretch, but he remembers.'

She listened to him with deep emotion. A tear started in the bell-ringer's eye, but it did not fall; he seemed to make it a point of honor to repress it.

'Listen,' he resumed, when he no longer feared that this tear would fall. 'We have here very high towers; a man who should fall from one would be dead before he touched the pavement; when it shall please you to have me to fall, you will not have to even utter a word; a glance will suffice.'

Then he rose. This odd being, unhappy as the gypsy was, still aroused some compassion in her breast. She motioned to him to remain.

'No, no,' said he, 'I must not stay too long, I am not at my ease. It is out of pity that you do not turn away your eyes. I will go where I can see you without you seeing me; it will be better so.'

He drew from his pocket a small metal whistle. 'There,' said he; 'when you want me, when you wish me to come, when you do not feel too much horror at the sight of me, use this whistle. I can hear this sound.'

He laid the whistle on the ground and fled.

4

Time went on.

Calm gradually returned to the soul of La Esmeralda. Excessive grief, like excessive joy, is a violent thing, which is of short duration. The human heart cannot long remain in either extremity. The gypsy had suffered so much that surprise was now the only emotion of which she was capable.

With the feeling of security, hope had returned to her. She was out of the pale of society, out of the pale of life; but she vaguely felt that it might not perhaps be impossible to return to them. She was like one dead, keeping in reserve a key to her tomb.

Thus each sunrise found her less pale, calmer, and breathing more freely. In proportion as her internal wounds healed, grace and beauty bloomed again on her countenance, but more retiring and composed. Her former character also returned – something even of her gaiety, her pretty pout, the fondness for her goat, her love of singing, her feminine bashfulness. She was careful to dress each morning in the corner of her little chamber, lest some inhabitant of the neighboring garrets should see her through her window.

When her thoughts of Phœbus allowed her leisure, the gypsy-girl sometimes thought of Quasimodo. He was the only link, the only means of communication with mankind, with the living, that remained to her. Poor child! She was even more out of the world than Quasimodo himself. She knew not what to make of the strange friend whom chance had given her. Often she reproached herself for not having a gratitude sufficient to shut her eyes; but, positively, she could not reconcile herself to the sight of the ringer; he was too ugly.

She had left the whistle he had given her lying upon the ground. This, however, did not prevent Quasimodo from reappearing, from time to time, during the first days. She strove hard to restrain herself from turning away with too strong an appearance of repugnance when he came to bring her the basket of provisions or the pitcher of water; but he always perceived the slightest motion of the kind, and went away sorrowful.

One day he came at the moment she was caressing Djali. For a while he stood, full of thought, before the graceful group of the goat and the gypsy; at length he said, shaking his heavy and mishapen head:

'My misfortune is, that I am still too much like a man – would that I were wholly a beast, like that goat.'

She raised her eyes toward him with a look of astonishment.

To this look he answered, 'Oh, I well know why!' and went his way.

At last, one morning, La Esmeralda had advanced to the verge of the roof, and was looking into the Place over the pointed roof of Saint-Jean-le-Rond. Quasimodo was there behind her. He used to so place himself of his own accord, in order to spare the young girl as much as possible the unpleasantness of seeing him. Suddenly the gypsy started; a tear and a flash of joy sparkled simultaneously in her eyes; she knelt down on the edge of the roof, and stretched out her arms in anguish toward the Place, crying out 'Phœbus! oh, come! come hither! One word! but one word, in heaven's name! Phœbus! Phœbus!'

Quasimodo leaned over and saw that the object of this tender and agonizing prayer was a young man, a captain, a handsome cavalier, glistening with arms and accoutrements, prancing across the end of the square, and saluting with his plume a beautiful young lady smiling at her balcony. The officer, however, did not hear the unhappy girl calling him, for he was too far off.

But the poor deaf man heard it. A deep sigh heaved his breast. He turned round. His heart was swollen with the tears which he repressed; his convulsively clenched fists struck against his head, and when he withdrew them there was in each of them a handful of red hair.

The gypsy was paying no attention to him. He said, in an undertone, grinding his teeth:

'Damnation! That is how one ought to look, then! One need but have a handsome outside!'

Meanwhile she remained kneeling, crying with extraordinary agitation.

The deaf man was watching her. He understood this pantomime. The poor ringer's eye filled with tears, but he let none fall. All at once he pulled her gently by the border of her sleeve. She turned round. He had assumed a look of composure, and said to her: 'Shall I go and fetch him?'

She uttered a cry of joy.

'Oh, go! go! Run! quick! – that captain, that captain! bring him to me! I will love thee!'

She clasped his knees. He could not help shaking his head sorrowfully.

'I will bring him to you,' said he, in a faint voice. Then he turned his head, and plunged hastily down the staircase, his heart bursting with sobs.

When he reached the Place, he found only the handsome horse fastened at the door of the Gondelaurier mansion; the captain had just gone in.

He looked up at the roof of the church. La Esmeralda was still there, on the same spot in the same posture. He made her a melancholy sign of the head; then set his back against one of the posts of the porch of the mansion, determined to wait until the captain should come forth.

In the Gondelaurier house it was one of those gala days which preceded a marriage. Quasimodo saw many people enter, and no one came out. From time to time he looked up at the roof of the church; the gypsy did not stir any more than he. A groom came and untied the horse, and led him to the stable of the household.

The entire day passed thus – Quasimodo against the post, La Esmeralda upon the roof, Phœbus, no doubt, at the feet of Fleur-de-Lys.

At length night came; a dark, moonless night. In vain did Quasimodo fix his gaze upon La Esmeralda; she was but a white spot in the twilight, then nothing was to be seen. All had vanished, all was black.

Quasimodo saw the front windows from top to bottom of the Gondelaurier mansion illuminated. He saw the other casements in the Place lighted one by one; he also saw them extinguished to the very last, for he remained the whole evening at his post. The officer did not come forth. When the last passers-by had returned home, when the windows of all the other houses were in darkness, Quasimodo remained entirely alone, entirely in the dark. There were at that time no lamps in the square of Notre-Dame.

Towards one o'clock in the morning the guests began to take their leave. Quasimodo, wrapped in darkness, watched them all pass out through the porch; none of them was the captain.

He was full of melancholy thoughts; at times he looked up into the air, like one weary of waiting. Great black clouds, heavy, torn, split, hung like ragged festoons of crape beneath the starry arch of night.

In one of those moments he suddenly saw the long folding window that opened upon the balcony, whose stone balustrade projected above his head, mysteriously open. The frail glass door gave passage to two persons, then closed noiselessly behind them. It was not without difficulty that Quasimodo, in the dark, recognized in the man the handsome captain, in the woman, the young lady whom he had seen in the morning welcoming the officer from that very balcony. The square was quite dark, and a double crimson curtain, which had fallen behind the glass door the moment it closed, allowed no light to reach the balcony from the apartment.

The young man and the young girl, as far as our deaf man could judge without hearing a word they said, appeared to abandon themselves to a very tender tête-à-tête. The young lady seemed to have permitted the officer to make a girdle for her waist of his arm, and was gently resisting a kiss.

Quasimodo looked on from below this scene, all the more interesting to witness, as it was not intended to be seen. He contemplated, with bitterness, that happiness, that beauty. After all, nature was not silent in the poor fellow, and his vertebral column, wretchedly distorted as it was, quivered no less than another's. He thought of the miserable portion which Providence had allotted to him; that woman, love and its pleasures, would pass forever before his eyes without his ever doing anything but witness the felicity of others. But what pained him most of all in this spectacle, what mingled indignation with his chagrin, was the thought of what the gypsy would suffer could she behold it.

Meanwhile their conversation grew more and more animated. The young lady seemed to be entreating the officer to ask nothing more from her. Quasimodo could only distinguish the fair clasped hands, the mingled smiles and tears, the young girl's glances directed to the stars, and the eyes of the captain lowered ardently upon her.

Fortunately, for the young girl was beginning to resist but feebly, the door of the balcony suddenly reopened, and an old lady made her appearance; the young beauty looked confused, the officer annoyed, and all three went in.

A moment later a horse was prancing under the porch, and the brilliant officer, enveloped in his night cloak, passed rapidly before Quasimodo.

The bell-ringer allowed him to turn the corner of the street, then ran after him, with his ape-like agility, shouting: 'Hi! captain!'

The captain halted.

'What does the rascal want with me?' said he, espying in the dark that uncouth figure running toward him limping.

Quasimodo, however, had come up to him, and boldly taken his horse by the bridle: 'Follow me, captain; there is one here who desires to speak with you.'

'By Mahound's horns,' grumbled Phœbus, 'here's a villainous ragged bird that I fancy I've seen somewhere. Hello! sirrah! leave hold of my horse's bridle!'

'Captain,' answered the deaf man, 'do you not ask me who it is?'

'I tell thee to let go my horse,' returned Phœbus, impatiently. 'What means the rogue hanging thus from my bridle rein?'

Quasimodo, far from releasing the bridle, was preparing to make him turn round. Unable to comprehend the captain's resistance, he hastened to say to him:

'Come, captain; 'tis a woman who is waiting for you.' He added, with an effort, 'a woman who loves you.'

'A rare varlet!' said the captain, 'who thinks me obliged to go after every woman that loves me, or says she does – and if perchance she resembles thee with thy face of a screech-owl? Tell her that sent thee that I am going to be married, and that she may go to the devil.'

'Hark ye!' cried Quasimodo, thinking to overcome his hesitation with a word; 'come, monseigneur; 'tis the gypsy-girl that you know of.'

This word did, in fact, make a great impression on Phœbus, but not that which the deaf man expected. It will be remembered that our gallant officer had retired with Fleur-de-Lys several moments before Quasimodo had rescued the condemned girl from the hands of Charmolue. Since then, in all his visits at the Logis Gondelaurier, he had taken care not to mention that woman, the recollection of whom was besides painful to him; and Fleur-de-Lys, on her part, had not deemed it politic to tell him that the gypsy was alive. Hence, Phœbus believed poor *Similar* dead a month or two ago. Add to this, for some moments the captain had been thinking of the extreme darkness of the night, the supernatural ugliness and sepulchral voice of the strange messenger; that it was past midnight; that the street was as solitary as the night that the spectre monk had accosted him, and that his horse panted as it looked at Quasimodo.

'The gypsy!' he exclaimed, almost frightened. 'How now! Art thou come from the other world?' And he laid his hand on the hilt of his dagger.

'Quick! quick!' said the deaf man, endeavoring to drag the horse along; 'this way!'

Phœbus dealt him a vigorous kick in the breast.

Quasimodo's eye flashed. He made a movement as if to fling himself upon the captain. Then, checking himself, he said:

'Oh, how happy you are to have some one who loves you!'

Phœbus spurred on in all haste, swearing. Quasimodo watched him disappear in the misty darkness of the street.

'Oh!' said the poor deaf creature to himself, 'to refuse that!'

He returned to Notre-Dame, lighted his lamp, and climbed

137

up the tower again. As he expected, the gypsy-girl was still at the same spot.

The moment she perceived he was coming she ran to meet him.

'Alone!' she cried, clasping her pretty hands in anguish.

'I could not find him again,' said Quasimodo coldly.

'You should have waited for him all night,' returned she passionately.

He saw her angry gesture, and understood the reproof.

'I'll watch him better another time,' said he, hanging his head.

'Get you gone,' said she.

He left her. She was dissatisfied with him. He would have preferred being chided by her than to cause her pain. He had kept all the grief for himself.

From that day forward the gypsy saw him no more; he ceased coming to her cell. Now and then, indeed, she caught a distant glimpse of the ringer's countenance looking mournfully upon her from the top of some tower; but as soon as she perceived him, he would disappear.

We must admit that she was but little troubled by the voluntary absence of the poor hunchback. At the bottom of her heart she felt grateful to him for it. Nor was Quasimodo himself under any delusion upon this point.

She saw him no more, but she felt the presence of a good genius about her. Her provisions were renewed by an invisible hand while she slept. One morning she found upon her window-sill a cage of birds. Over her cell there was a piece of sculpture that frightened her. She had repeatedly evinced this feeling in Quasimodo's presence. One morning (for all these things were done in the night) she saw it no longer; it had been broken off. He who had climbed to that piece of carving must have risked his life.

On waking one morning, she saw in her window two jars full of flowers; one of them a glass vessel, very beautiful and brilliant, but cracked; it had let all the water escape, and the flowers it contained were faded. The other vessel was of earthenware, rude and common, but it had kept the water, so that its flowers were fresh and blooming.

I do not know whether she did it intentionally, but La Esmeralda took the faded nosegay and wore it all day in her bosom.

That day she did not hear the voice from the tower singing.

She felt little concern about it. She passed her days in caressing Djali, watching the door of the Logis Gondelaurier, in talking low to herself about Phœbus, and crumbling her bread to the swallows.

She had altogether ceased to see or to hear Quasimodo. The poor ringer seemed to have departed from the church. One night, however, as she lay wakeful, thinking of her handsome captain, she heard a sigh, near to her cell. She rose up affrighted, and saw, by the moonlight, a shapeless mass lying before her door. It was Quasimodo sleeping there upon the stones.

5

Meanwhile public rumor had acquainted the archdeacon with the miraculous manner in which the gypsy-girl had been saved. When he learned this, he felt he knew not what. He had reconciled his mind to the thought of La Esmeralda's death, and thus he had become calm; he had touched the depths of possible grief.

Now, Esmeralda being dead, all was over for Dom Claude upon this earth. But to feel that she was alive, and Phœbus also – that was the recommencement of torture, of pangs, of vicissitudes, of life – and Dom Claude was weary of all that.

When this piece of intelligence reached him, he shut himself in his cloister cell. He appeared neither at the conferences of the chapter, nor at the services in the church. He closed his door against everyone, even the bishop. He kept himself thus immured for several weeks. He was thought to be ill, and so indeed he was.

He passed whole days with his face pressed against the casement of his window. From that window, situated in the cloister, he could see the cell of Esmeralda; he often saw herself, with her goat – sometimes with Quasimodo. He remarked the assiduities of the ugly deaf man, his obedience, his delicate and submissive behavior to the gypsy-girl. He recollected – for he had a good memory, and memory is the tormentor of the jealous – he recollected the singular look which the ringer had cast upon the dancing-girl on a certain evening. He asked himself what motive could have urged Quasimodo to save her. He was an eye-witness to a thousand little scenes which passed between the gypsy and the ringer; were, in their gestures, as seen at that distance and commented on by his passion, appeared to him most tender. He distrusted woman's capriciousness. Then he felt confusedly arising within him a jealousy such as he had never imagined; a jealousy which made him redden with shame and indignation.

His nights were frightful. Since he knew the gypsy-girl to be alive, those cold images of spectres and the grave, which had beset him for a whole day, had vanished from his spirit, and the flesh began again to torment him. He writhed upon his bed at the thought that the dark-skinned damsel was so near him.

Each night his delirious imagination represented to him La Esmeralda in all the attitudes that had most strongly excited his passion. He beheld her stretched across the body of the poniarded captain, her eyes closed, her fair neck crimsoned with the blood of Phœbus; at that moment of wild delight when the archdeacon had imprinted on her pale lips that kiss of which the unfortunate girl, half dying as she was, had felt the burning pressure. Again he beheld her undressed by the savage hands of the torturers, letting them thrust her little foot naked into the horrid iron-screwed buskin, her round and delicate leg, her white and supple knee; and then he saw that ivory knee alone appearing, all below it being enveloped in Torterue's horrible apparatus. He figured to himself the young girl, in her slight chemise, with the rope about her neck, with bare feet and uncovered shoulders, almost naked, as he had seen her upon the last day. These voluptuous images made him clench his hands, and sent a shiver through his frame.

One night in particular, they so cruelly inflamed his priestly virgin blood, that he tore his pillow with his teeth, leaped from bed, threw a surplice over his night-robe, and went out of his cell with his lamp in hand, half naked, wild, with flaming eyes.

He knew where to find the key of the red door, opening from the cloister into the church; and, as the reader is aware, he always carried about him a key of the tower staircase.

6

That night La Esmeralda had fallen asleep in her little chamber, full of forgetfulness, of hope and of happy thoughts. She had been sleeping some time, dreaming, as usual, of Phœbus, when she thought she heard some noise about her. Her sleep was light and restless – the sleep of a bird; the slightest thing awakened her. She opened her eyes. The night was very dark. Yet she discerned at the little window a face regarding her; there was a lamp which cast its light upon this apparition. The moment that it perceived itself to be observed by La Esmeralda, it blew out the lamp. Nevertheless, the young girl had caught a glimpse of its features; her eyelids dropped with terror. 'Oh!' said she in a faint voice, 'the priest!'

A moment after, she felt a contact the whole length of her body, which made her shudder so violently that she started up in bed wide awake and furious. The priest had glided to her side and clasped her in his arms.

She strove to cry out, but could not.

'Begone, monster! begone, assassin!' said she, in a voice low and faltering with anger and horror.

'Mercy! mercy!' murmured the priest, pressing his lips to her shoulders.

She seized his bald head with both her hands by the remaining hairs, and strove to repel his kisses, as if he had been biting her.

'Mercy!' repeated the wretched man. 'Didst thou but know what is my love for thee! 'Tis fire! 'tis molten lead! 'tis a thousand daggers in my heart!'

And he held back both her arms with superhuman strength. Quite desperate, 'Let me go,' she cried, 'or I spit in thy face!'

'Love me! love me! have pity!' cried the poor priest, rolling upon her and answering her blows with caresses.

All at once she felt that he was overpowering her. 'There must be an end of this,' said he, grinding his teeth.

She was conquered, crushed and quivering in his arms. She felt a lascivious hand wandering over her. She made a last effort, and shrieked: 'Help! help me! A vampire! a vampire!'

But nothing came. Only Djali was awake and bleated piteously.

'Silence!' said the panting priest.

Suddenly, in the midst of her struggles, as the gypsy retreated upon the floor, her hand came in contact with something cold and metallic. It was Quasimodo's whistle. She seized it with a convulsion of hope, put it to her lips, and blew with all her remaining strength. The whistle sounded clear, shrill, piercing.

'What is that?' said the priest.

Almost at the same instant he felt himself lifted by a vigorous arm. The cell was dark; he could not clearly distinguish who it was that held him thus; but he heard teeth clenching with rage, and there was just light enough mingled with the darkness for him to see shining over his head a large cutlass.

The priest thought he could discern the form of Quasimodo. He supposed it could be no other. He recollected having stumbled, in entering, over a bundle that was lying across the doorway outside. Yet, as the new-comer uttered no word, he knew not what to think. He threw himself upon the arm that held the cutlass, crying, 'Quasimodo!' forgetting, in that moment of distress, that Quasimodo was deaf.

In the twinkling of an eye the priest was thrown upon the floor, and felt a knee of lead weighing upon his breast. By the angular imprint of that knee he recognized Quasimodo. But what was he to do? how was he to make himself known to the other? Night made the deaf man blind.

He was lost. The young girl, devoid of pity, as an enraged tigress, did not interfere to save him. The cutlass approached his head; the moment was critical. Suddenly his adversary appeared to hesitate. 'No blood upon her!' said he, in an undertone.

It was, in fact, the voice of Quasimodo.

Then the priest felt the great hand dragging him by the foot out of the cell; it was there he was to die. Luckily for him, the moon had been risen for a few moments.

When they had cleared the door of the chamber, its pale rays fell upon the features of the priest. Quasimodo looked in his face; a tremor came over him; he relaxed his hold of the priest and shrank back.

The gypsy having come forward to the threshold of her cell, was surprised to see them suddenly change parts; for now it was the priest who threatened, and Quasimodo who implored.

The deaf man bowed his head, then came and knelt before the gypsy's door. 'Monseigneur,' said he, in a tone of gravity and resignation, 'afterwards you will do what you please, but kill me first.'

So saying, he presented his cutlass to the priest; and the priest, beside himself, rushed forward to grasp it; but the girl was quicker than he. She snatched the cutlass from Quasimodo's hand, and burst into a frantic laugh. 'Approach!' said she to the priest.

She held the blade aloft. The priest hesitated. She would certainly have struck. 'Thou durst not approach now, coward!' she exclaimed. Then she added, in a pitiless accent, and well knowing that it would be plunging a red-hot iron into the heart of the priest: 'Ha! I know that Phœbus is not dead!'

The priest overthrew Quasimodo with a kick, and plunged, trembling with rage, under the vault of the staircase.

When he had gone, Quasimodo picked up the whistle that had just saved the gypsy. 'It was growing rusty,' said he, as he gave it to her, and then he left her alone.

The young girl, overpowered by this violent scene, fell exhausted upon her couch, and burst into a flood of tears. Again her horizon was growing overcast.

As for the priest, he had groped his way back into his cell.

'Twas done. Dom Claude was jealous of Quasimodo. He repeated pensively to himself his fatal sentence: 'No one shall have her!'

BOOK EIGHT

1

From the time that Pierre Gringoire had seen the turn that this affair was taking, and that torture, hanging and various other disagreeables were decidedly in store for the principal personages in this comedy, he no longer felt any desire to take part in it. The Truands, amongst whom he had remained, considering that, after all, they were the best company in Paris – the Truands had continued to feel interested in the gypsy. This he found very natural in people who, like herself, had nothing but Charmolue and Torterue in prospect, and who did not, like himself, soar into the regions of imagination between the two wings of Pegasus. He had learned from their discourse that his bride of the broken pitcher had found refuge in Notre-Dame, and he was glad of it. But he did not even feel tempted to go and see her there. He sometimes thought of the little goat, and that was all.

One day he had stopped near the church of Saint-Germain-l'Auxerrois, at the corner of a building called *le For-l'Evêque*, which was opposite another called *le For-le-Roi*.

All at once, he felt a hand fall heavily on his shoulder; he turned round – it was his old friend, his old master, monsieur, the archdeacon.

He was quite confounded. It was long since he had seen the archdeacon; and Dom Claude was one of those grave and ardent beings, a meeting with whom always disturbs the equilibrium of a sceptical philosopher.

The archdeacon maintained silence for some moments, during which Gringoire had leisure to observe him. He found Dom Claude much altered, pale as a winter morning, with hollow eyes and hair almost white. The priest was the first to break this silence, by saying in a calm but freezing tone: 'How do you do, Maître Pierre?'

'As to my health,' answered Gringoire, 'eh! eh! one can say both one thing and another on that score. Still it is good, on the whole. I do not take too much of anything.'

Dom Claude interrupted him: 'You are happy, then?'

Gringore replied with conviction: 'On my honor, yes! First,

I loved women, then animals; now I love stones. They are quite as amusing as animals or women and less treacherous.'

After a short silence, the priest resumed:

'You are, nevertheless, poor enough?'

'Poor? Yes, but not unhappy.'

'Come hither,' said the priest; 'I have something to say to you.'

Gringoire followed him, being wont to obey him, like all who had once approached that commanding personality. They reached in silence the Rue des Bernardins, which was almost deserted. Dom Claude stopped.

'What have you to say to me, master?' asked Gringoire.

'Pierre Gringoire,' said the archdeacon, 'what have you done with that little gypsy dancer?'

'Esmeralda? You change the conversation very abruptly.'

'Was she not your wife?'

'Yes, by virtue of a broken pitcher. We were in for it for four years. By-the-by,' added Gringoire, looking at the archdeacon with a half-bantering air, 'you think of her still, then?'

'And you – do you no longer think of her?'

'Very little. I have so many things! Good heavens! how pretty the little goat was!'

'Did not that Bohemian girl save your life?'

'' Tis true, pardieu.'

'Well, what became of her? what have you done with her?'

'I was told she had taken refuge in Notre-Dame, and that she was there in safety; and I am delighted at it; and I have not been able to discover whether the goat escaped with her, and that is all I know about the matter.'

'I will tell you more,' cried Dom Claude; and his voice, till then low, deliberate and hollow, became like thunder. 'She has, indeed, taken refuge in Notre-Dame. But in three days justice will drag her again from thence, and she will be hanged at the Grève. There is a decree of the Parliament for it!'

'Now, that is a shame,' said Gringoire.

The priest in a moment had become cool and calm again.

'And who the devil,' continued the poet, 'has taken the trouble to solicit a decree of reintegration? Could they not leave the Parliament alone? Or what consequence can it be that a poor girl takes shelter under the buttresses of Notre-Dame, among the swallows' nests?'

'There are Satans in the world,' answered the archdeacon.

'That's a devillish bad piece of work,' observed Gringoire.

The archdeacon resumed, after a short silence:

'So then, she saved your life?'

'Yes, among my good friends the Truands. I was within an

144

inch of being hanged. They would have been sorry for it now.'

'Will you not do something for her, then?'

'I should rejoice to be of service, Dom Claude; but if I were to bring a bad piece of business about my ears!'

'What can it signify?'

'The deuce! what can it signify! You are very kind, master! I have two great works begun.'

'She must leave there, nevertheless,' murmured he. 'The decree is to be put in force within three days. Otherwise, it would not be valid. That Quasimodo! Women have very depraved tastes!' He raised his voice: 'Maître Pierre, I have well considered the matter. There is but one means of saving her.'

'And what is it? For my part, I see none.'

'Hark ye, Maître Pierre; remember that you owe your life to her. I will tell you candidly my idea. The church is watched day and night; no one is allowed to come out but those who have been seen to go in. Thus you can go in. You shall come, and I will take you to her. You will change clothes with her. She will take your doublet, and you will take her petticoat.'

'So far, so good,' observed the philosopher; 'and what then?'

'What then? Why, she will go out in your clothes, and you will remain in hers. You may get hanged, perhaps, but she will be saved.'

Gringoire scratched his ear with a very serious air.

'I say, master, that I shall not be hanged perhaps, but that I shall be hanged indubitably.'

'Maître Pierre, it must absolutely be so.' The archdeacon spoke imperiously.

'Hark you, Dom Claude,' answered the poet, in great consternation. 'You hold to that idea, and you are wrong. I don't see why I should get myself hanged instead of another.'

The archdeacon held out his hand to him, 'You will come tomorrow?'

''Faith, no!' said he. 'To get hanged! 'tis too absurd. I will not.'

'Farewell, then;' and the archdeacon added between his teeth, 'I will find thee again.'

'I do not want that devil of a man to find me again,' thought Gringoire; and he ran after Dom Claude. 'Stay, monsieur the archdeacon,' said he; 'old friends should not fall out. You take an interest in that girl – my wife, I mean. 'Tis well. You have devised a scheme for getting her out of Notre-Dame; but your plan is extremely unpleasant for me, Gringoire. Now, if I could suggest another, myself! – I beg to say, a most luminous inspiration has just occurred to me. If I had an expedient for extracting her from her sorry plight, without compromising my neck in the smallest degree with a slip-knot, what would you say? would not that suffice you? Must I absolutely be hanged before you are content?'

And Gringoire and the archdeacon agreed on an ingenious and bloody plan, to take place soon.

2

A few nights later Quasimodo slept not. He had just gone his last round through the church. He had not noticed, at the moment when he was closing the doors, that the archdeacon had passed near him and had displayed some degree of ill-humor at seeing him bolt and padlock with care the enormous iron bars which gave to these closed portals the solidity of a wall. Dom Claude appeared even more preoccupied than usual. Moreover, since the nocturnal adventure of the cell, he was constantly ill-treating Quasimodo; but in vain he used him harshly, even striking him sometimes; nothing could shake the submission, the patience, the devoted resignation of the faithful ringer. From the archdeacon he could endure anything – insults, threats, blows – without murmuring a reproach, without uttering a complaint. At most he would follow Dom Claude anxiously with his eye, as he ascended the staircase of the towers; but the archdeacon had of himself abstained from again appearing before the gypsy-girl.

On that night, accordingly, Quasimodo, after casting one look toward his poor forsaken bells, mounted to the top of the northern tower, and there, placing his well-closed dark-lantern on the leads, took a survey of Paris. The night, as we have already said, was very dark. Paris, which, comparatively speaking, was not lighted at that period, presented to the eye a confused heap of black masses, intersected here and there by the whitish curve of the Seine.

While his only eye was thus hovering over that horizon of mist and darkness, the ringer felt within him an inexpressible uneasiness. For several days he had been upon the watch. He had seen constantly wandering around the church men of sinister aspect, who never took their eyes from the young girl's asylum. He feared lest some plot might be hatching against the unfortunate well as himself, and that something sinister might probably happen soon. All at once, while he was reconnoitring the great city with that eye which nature, as if by way of compensation, had made so piercing that it almost supplied the deficiency of other organs in Quasimodo, it struck him that there was something unusual in the appearance of the outline of the quay of the Vielle-Pelleterie, that there was some movement at that point.

This appeared strange to him. He redoubled his attention. The movement appeared to be towards the city. No light was to be seen. It remained some time on the quay, then flowed off it by degrees, as if whatever was passing along was entering the interior of the island; then it ceased entirely, and the line of the quay became straight and motionless again.

Just as Quasimodo was exhausting himself in conjectures, it seemed to him that the movement was reappearing in the Rue du Parvis. In fact, notwithstanding the great darkness, he could see the head of a column issuing from that street, and in an instant a crowd spreading over the square, of which he could distinguish nothing further than that it was a crowd.

Then his fears returned. Should he awaken the Egyptian? assist her to escape? Which way? The streets were beset; behind the church was the river; there was no boat, no egress! There was but one measure to be taken: to meet death on the threshold of Notre-Dame; to resist at least until some assistance came, if any were to come, and not to disturb the sleep of Esmeralda. The unhappy girl would be awakened soon enough to die. This resolution once taken, he proceeded to reconnoitre the *enemy* more calmly.

The crowd seemed to be increasing every moment in the Parvis. He concluded, however, that very little noise was made, since the windows of the streets and the square remained closed. All at once a light flashed up, and in an instant seven or eight lighted torches were waving above the heads. Quasimodo then saw distinctly surging, in the Parvis, a frightful troop of men and women in rags, armed with scythes, pikes, pruning-hooks, partisans, the thousand points of which all glittered. Here and there black pitchforks formed horns to those hideous visages. He had a confused recollection of that populace, and thought he recognized all the heads which, a few months before, had saluted him Pope of the Fools. A man holding a torch in one hand and a club in the other mounted a stone post and appeared to be haranguing them. At the same time the strange army performed some evolutions, as if taking post around the church.

Clopin Trouillefou, King of the Truands, having arrived before the principal door of Notre-Dame, had, in fact, ranged his troops in order of battle. Although he did not anticipate any resistance, yet, like a prudent general, he wished to preserve such a degree of order as would, in case of need, enable him to face a sudden attack of the watch or of the guardsmen.

When the first arrangements were completed – and we must say, to the honor of Truand discipline, that Clopin's orders were executed in silence and with admirable precision – the worthy leader mounted the parapet of the Parvis, and raised his hoarse and surly voice, his face turned toward Notre-Dame, and brandishing his torch, whose flame, tossed by the wind and veiled at intervals by its own smoke, made the glowing front of the church by turns appear and disappear before the eye:

'Forward, my sons!' cried he. 'To your work, locksmiths.'

Thirty stout men, fellows with brawny limbs and the faces of blacksmiths, sprang from the ranks, with hammers, pincers and iron crows on their shoulders. They advanced toward the principal door of the church; ascended the steps; and directly they were to be seen stooping down under the pointed arches of the portal, heaving at the door with pincers and levers.

The door, however, stood firm.

'Courage, my friends!' cried Clopin. 'I'll wager my head against a slipper that you'll have burst the door, taken the girl, and undressed the great altar, before there is one beadle awake. Stay! I think the lock is giving way.'

Clopin was interrupted by a frightful noise which at that moment resounded behind him. He turned round; an enormous beam had just fallen from on high, crushing a dozen of the Truands upon the church steps, and rebounding upon the pavement with the sound of a piece of artillery; breaking legs here and there in the crowd of vagabonds who sprang aside with cries of terror. In a twinkling the narrow precincts of the Parvis were cleared. The locksmiths, though protected by the deer arches of the portal, abandoned the door, and Clopin himself fell back to a respectful distance from the church.

It is impossible to describe the astonishment mixed with dread which fell upon the bandits with this beam. They remained for some minutes gazing fixedly upward, in greater consternation at this piece of wood than they would have been at twenty thousand king's archers.

Nothing was distinguishable upon the grand front of the building, to the top of which the light from the torches did not reach. The ponderous piece of timber lay in the middle of the Parvis; and groans were heard from the miserable wretches who had received its first shock, and been almost cut in two upon the angles of the stone steps.

At last the King of Tunis, his first astonishment over, hit upon an explanation which his comrades thought plausible.

'God's throat!' said he, 'are the canons making a defense? To the sack, then! to the sack!'

'To the sack!' repeated the mob with a furious hurrah. And they made a general discharge of cross-bows and hackbuts against the front of the church.

The King of Tunis ran bravely up to the formidable piece of timber, and set his foot upon it. 'Here's the battering ram we need!' cried he; 'the canons have sent it to you.'

This bravado had great effect; the spell of the wonderful beam was broken. The Truands recovered courage; and soon the heavy timber, picked up like a feather by two hundred vigorous arms, was driven with fury against the great door.

At the shock given by the beam, the half metal door sounded like an immense drum. It was not burst in, but the whole cathedral shook, and in its deepest recesses could be heard rumblings. At the same moment, a shower of great stones began to fall from the upper part of the façade upon the assailants.

It must be remarked that these stones all fell one by one; but they followed one another closely. The Argotiers always felt two of them at one and the same time, one against their legs, the other upon their heads. Nearly all of them took effect; and already the dead and wounded were thickly strewn, bleeding and panting under the feet of the assailants, who, now grown furious, filled up instantly and without intermission the places of the disabled. The long beam continued battering the door with periodical strokes, like the clapper of a bell, the stones to shower down, the door to groan.

The reader has undoubtedly not waited till this time to divine that this unexpected resistance which had exasperated the Truands proceeded from Quasimodo.

All at once, at the moment that they were crowding about the battering-ram for a final effort, each one holding in his breath and stiffening his muscles, so as to give full force to the decisive stroke, a howl more frightful still than that which had burst forth and expired beneath the beam, arose from the midst of them. Those who did not cry out, those who were still alive, looked. Two jets of melted lead were falling from the top of the edifice into the thickest of the rabble. That sea of men had gone down under the boiling metal, which, at the two points where it fell, had made two black and smoking holes in the crowd, like hot water thrown on snow. There were to be seen dying wretches burned half to a cinder, and moaning with agony.

The outcry was heart-rending. They fled in disorder, hurling the beam upon the dead bodies.

All eyes were raised to the top of the church. They beheld there

149

an extraordinary sight. On the crest of the highest gallery, higher than the central rose window, was a great flame ascending between the two towers, with whirlwinds of sparks; a great flame, irregular and furious, a tongue of which, by the action of the wind, was at times borne into the smoke. Underneath that flame, two monster-headed gutters were vomiting incessantly that burning shower, whose silver stream shone out against the darkness of the lower façade.

A terrified silence ensued among the Truands; during which nothing was heard but the cries of alarm from the canons, shut up in their cloisters and more uneasy than horses in a burning stable.

Meanwhile the principal Truands had retired beneath the porch of the Logis Gondelaurier, and were holding a council of war. Clopin Trouillefou was gnawing his huge fists with rage.

'Impossible to get in!' muttered he between his teeth.

'Do you see that demon, going back and forth before the fire?' cried the Duke of Egypt.

'Par-Dieu!' said Clopin, 'tis the damned ringer – 'tis Quasimodo. Is there then no way of forcing this door?' continued the King of Tunis, stamping his foot. 'Must we then slink away pitifully, like so many running footmen?' said Clopin. 'What! leave our sister there, for those hooded wolves to hang tomorrow!'

'And the sacristy – where there are cartloads of gold!' added another rascal.

'Who's for it?' said Clopin. 'I'll go at it again. By-the-by, where's Maître Pierre Gringoire?'

'Captain Clopin,' said Andry-le-Rouge, 'he slipped away before we had got as far as the Pont-aux-Changeurs.'

Clopin stamped his foot. 'Gueule-Dieu! 'Tis he who pushed us on hither, and then leaves us here just in the thick of the job. Cowardly chatterer, with a slipper for a helmet!'

'Captain Clopin,' cried Andry-le-Rouge, looking up the Rue de Parvis, 'yonder comes the little student Jehan de Frollo!'

'Praise be to Pluto!' said Clopin. 'But what the devil is he dragging after him?'

It was in fact Jehan, who had joined the Truands after quarrelling with his brother, coming as quick as he found practicable under his ponderous knightly accoutrements, with a long ladder, which he was dragging stoutly over the pavement.

'Victory! Te Deum!' shouted the student. 'Here's the ladder belonging to the unloaders of Saint Laundry's wharf.'

Clopin went up to him.

'Child, what are you going to do, corne-Dieu! with this ladder?'

'What am I going to do with it, august King of Tunis?' said

he. 'Do you see that row of statues there, that look like block-heads, over the three portals?'

'Yes. Well?'

At the end of that gallery there's a door that's always on the latch. With this ladder I reach it, and I am in the church.'

'Boy, let me go first.'

'No, comrade; the ladder is mine. Come, you shall be the second.'

'Beezelbub strangle thee!' said surly Clopin. 'I'll be second to no one.'

'Then, Clopin, find a ladder.'

Jehan set off on a run across the Place, dragging his ladder, and shouting: 'Follow me, boys!'

In an instant the ladder was raised and placed against the balustrade of the lower gallery, over one of the side doorways. The crowd of Truands, uttering loud acclamations, pressed to the foot of it for the purpose of ascending. But Jehan maintained his right, and was the first to set foot on the steps of the ladder.

The Truands followed him. There was one upon each step of the ladder.

The student at length reached the parapet of the gallery, and sprang lightly over it, amid the applause of the whole Truandry. Thus master of the citadel, he uttered a joyful shout, but stopped short, suddenly petrified. He had just discovered, concealed behind one of the royal statues, Quasimodo, his eye glittering in the shadow.

Before another of the besiegers had time to gain foothold on the gallery, the formidable hunchback sprang to the head of the ladder, seized, without saying a word, the ends of the two uprights with his powerful hands; heaved them away from the edge of the balustrade; balanced for a moment, amid cries of anguish, the long bending ladder, crowded with Truands from top to bottom; then suddenly, with superhuman strength, he threw back that clustering mass of men into the square.

A mingled murmur of pain and resentment among the besiegers succeeded their first shouts of triumph. Quasimodo, unmoved, his elbows resting upon the balustrade, was quietly looking on, with the mien of some old long-haired king looking out at his window.

Jehan Frollo, on the other hand, was in a critical situation. He found himself in the gallery with the redoubtable ringer – alone, separated from his companions by eighty feet of perpendicular wall. While Quasimodo was dealing with the ladder, the student had run to the postern, which he expected to find on the latch. Not so. The ringer, upon entering the gallery, had fastened it behind him. Jehan had then hidden himself behind one of the stone kings, not daring to draw breath, but fixing upon the monstrous hunchback a look of wild apprehension.

For the first few moments the hunchback took no notice of him; but at length he turned his head and stared, for the scholar had just caught his eye.

Jehan prepared for a rude encounter, but his deaf antagonist remained motionless; he had only turned toward the scholar, at whom he continued looking.

'Ho, ho!' said Jehan, 'why dost thou look at me with that one melancholy eye of thine?'

And so saying, the young rogue was stealthily adjusting his crossbow.

'Quasimodo,' he cried, 'I'm going to change thy surname. They shall call thee the blind.'

The arrow parted and whistled through the air, burying its point into the left arm of the hunchback. This no more disturbed Quasimodo than a scratch would have done his stone neighbor, King Pharamond. He laid his hand to the dart, drew it out of his arm, and quietly broke it over his big knee. Then he dropped, rather than threw, the two pieces on the ground. But he did not give Jehan time to discharge a second shaft. The arrow broken, Quasimodo, breathing heavily, bounded like a grasshopper upon the scholar, whose armor was flattened against the wall by the shock.

Quasimodo grasped in his left hand both the arms of Jehan, who made no struggle, so completely did he give himself up for lost. With his right hand the hunchback took off, one after another, with ominous deliberation, the several pieces of his armor — the sword, the daggers, the helmet, the breastplate, the arm-pieces — as if it had been a monkey peeling a walnut. Quasimodo dropped at his feet, piece after piece, the scholar's iron shell.

When the scholar had found himself disarmed and undressed, feeble and naked, in those terrible hands, he did not offer to speak to his deaf enemy; but he fell to laughing audaciously in his face, and singing, with the careless assurance of a boy of sixteen, a popular air of the time.

He did not finish. Quasimodo was seen standing upon the parapet of the gallery, holding the scholar by the feet with one hand only, and swinging him round like a sling over the abyss. Then a noise was heard like a box made of bone dashing against a wall; and something was seen falling, which stopped a third part of the way down, being arrested in its descent by one of the architectural projections. It was a dead body which hung there, bent double, the loins broken, and the skull empty.

A cry of horror arose from the Truands.

'Vengeance!' cried Clopin. 'Sack!' answered the multitude. 'Assault! assault!'

Then there was a prodigious howling, mixed with all languages, all dialects and all tones of voice. The poor student's death inspired the crowd with a frantic ardor. They were seized with shame and resentment at having been so long kept in check, before a church, by a hunchback. Their rage found them ladders, multiplied their torches, and in a few minutes Quasimodo, in confusion and despair, saw a frightful swarm ascending from all sides to the assault of Notre-Dame. Fury seemed to writhe in those ferocious countenances; their dirty foreheads streamed with perspiration; their eyes flashed; all these varieties of grimace and ugliness beset Quasimodo.

And Quasimodo, powerless against so many enemies, trembling for the gypsy, watched those furious faces approach nearer and nearer to his gallery, and implored a miracle from heaven, as he wrung his arms in despair.

3

Gringoire, on a secret mission of his own to the king, had just left the Bastille. When he had reached the Porte Baudoyer, he walked straight to the stone cross which rose in the middle of the open space there, as though he were able to discern in the dark the figure of a man clad and hooded in black, sitting upon the steps of the cross.

'Is it you, master?' said Gringoire.

The black figure started up.

'Death and passion! you make me boil, Gringoire. The man upon the tower of Saint Gervais has just cried half-past one in the morning!'

'Oh,' returned Gringoire, ' 'tis no fault of mine, but of the watch and the king. I have just had a narrow escape. I always just miss being hung. 'Tis my predestination.'

'You miss everything,' said the other. 'But come quickly. Have you the password?'

'I have it. Make yourself easy. *Petite flambe en baguenaud.*'

' 'Tis well. Otherwise we should not be able to reach the church. The rabble block up the streets. Fortunately, they seem to have met with resistance. We may, perhaps, still be there in time.'

'Yes, master; but how are we to get into Notre-Dame?'

'I have the key to the towers.'

'And how are we to get out again?'

'There is a small door behind the cloister, which leads to the Terrain, and so to the water-side. I have taken the key to it, and I moored a boat there this morning.'

Both then proceeded at a rapid pace towards the city.

4

The reader will, perhaps, recall the critical situation in which we left Quasimodo. The brave deaf man, assailed on all sides, had lost, if not all courage, at least all hope of saving, not himself — he thought not of himself — but the gypsy-girl. He ran distractedly along the gallery. Notre-Dame was on the point of being carried by the Truands. All at once a great galloping of horses filled the neighboring streets; and, with a long file of torches, and a dense column of horsemen, lances and bridles lowered, these furious sounds came rushing into the Place like a hurricane:

'France! France! Cut down the knaves! Chateaupers to the rescue! Provostry! provostry!'

The Truands in terror faced about.

Quasimodo, who heard nothing, saw the drawn swords, the flambeaux, the spear-heads, all that cavalry, at the head of which he recognized Captain Phœbus; he saw the confusion of the vagabonds, the terror of some of them, the perturbation of the stoutest-hearted among them, and this unexpected succor so much revived his own energies that he hurled back from the church the first assailants, who were already climbing into the gallery.

It was, in fact, the king's troops who had arrived.

The Truands bore themselves bravely. They defended themselves desperately.

The conflict was frightful. Wolves' flesh calls for dog's teeth, as Father Matthieu phrases it. The king's horsemen, amid whom Phœbus de Chateaupers bore himself valiantly, gave no quarter, and they who escaped the thrust of the lance fell by the edge of the sword. The Truands, ill-armed, foamed and bit with rage and despair. Men, women and children threw themselves upon the cruppers and chests of the horses, and clung to them like cats with tooth and nail.

At length the vagabonds gave way. Exhaustion, want of good weapons, the fright of this surprise, the discharges of musketry from the windows, and the spirited charge of the king's troops all combined to overpower them. They broke through the line of their assailants and fled in all directions, leaving the Parvis strewn with dead.

When Quasimodo, who had not for a moment ceased fighting, beheld this rout, he fell on his knees, and raised his hands to heaven. Then, intoxicated with joy, he ran, and ascended with the swiftness of a bird to that cell, the approaches to which he had so gallantly defended. He had now but one thought – it was to kneel before her whom he had just saved for the second time.

When he entered the cell he found it empty.

BOOK NINE

1

At the moment when the Truands had attacked the church Esmeralda was asleep.

Soon the ever-increasing uproar around the edifice, and the plaintive bleating of her goat, which awoke before her, roused her from her slumbers. She sat up, listened, and looked about her; then, frightened at the light and the noise, she had hurried from her cell to see what it was. The aspect of the square, the strange vision moving in it, the disorder of that nocturnal assault, that hideous crowd leaping like a cloud of frogs, half seen in the darkness; the croaking of that hoarse multitude, the few red torches dancing to and fro in the obscurity; all together seemed to her like some mysterious battle commenced between the phantoms of a witches' Sabbath and the stone monsters of the church.

By degrees, however, the first vapors of terror gradually dispersed; from the constantly increasing din, and from other signs of reality, she discovered that she was beset, not by spectres, but by human beings. Then her fear, though it did not increase, changed its nature. She had dreamed of the possibility of a popular rising to drag her from her asylum. The idea of once more losing life, hope, Phœbus, who still was ever present to her hopes; her extreme helplessness; all flight cut off, no support; her abandonment, her isolation; these thoughts and a thousand others had overwhelmed her. She had fallen upon her knees, with her head up on her couch, and her hands clasped upon her head, apprehensive and trembling.

In the midst of this anguish she heard a footstep close to her. She looked up. Two men, one of whom carried a lantern, had just entered her cell. She uttered a feeble cry.

'Fear nothing,' said a voice which was not unknown to her; ' 'tis I.'

'Who are you?' asked she.

'Pierre Gringoire.'

This name reassured her. She raised her eyes again and saw that it was indeed the poet. But there stood beside him a black figure, veiled from head to foot, the sight of which struck her dumb.

'Ah!' continued Gringoire, in a reproachful tone, 'Djali recognized me before you.'

The little goat, in fact, had not waited for Gringoire to announce himself. No sooner had he entered than it rubbed itself gently against his knees, covering the poet with caresses and white hairs, for it was shedding its coat. Gringoire returned the caresses.

'Who is that with you?' said the Egyptian, in a low tone.

'Do not be disturbed,' answered Gringoire; 'it is a friend of mine.'

They rapidly descended the staircase of the towers, crossed the interior of the church which was all dark and solitary, but reverberated from the uproar without; and went out by the red door into the courtyard of the cloister. The cloister was deserted, the canons having taken refuge in the bishop's house, there to offer up their prayers in common; the courtyard was empty, only some terrified serving-men were crouching in the darkest corners. They directed their steps towards the small door leading from this courtyard to the Terrain. The man in black opened it with a key which he had about him. Here, too, they found the tumult in the air sensibly diminished. The noise of the assault by the Truands reached their ears more confusedly and less clamorously.

The man with the lantern walked straight to the point of the Terrain. At the very brink of the water, there stood the worm-eaten remains of a fence of stakes with laths nailed across, upon which a low vine spread out its few meagre branches like the fingers of an open hand. Behind this sort of lattice-work, in the shadow which it cast, a small boat lay hidden. The man motioned to Gringoire and his companion to get in. The goat followed them. The man himself stepped in last of all. Then he cut the rope; pushed off from the shore with a long boat-hook, and laying hold of a pair of oars, seated himself in the bow, and rowed with all his might towards mid-stream. The Seine is very rapid at that point, and he found considerable difficulty in clearing the point of the island.

Gringoire's first care, on entering the boat was to place the goat on his knees. He took his seat in the stern; and the young girl, whom the stranger inspired with an indefinable uneasiness, seated herself as closely as possible to the poet.

The boat made its way slowly toward the right bank. The young girl watched the unknown with secret terror. He had carefully turned off the light of his dark lantern; he was now faintly seen, in the forepart of the skiff, like a spectre. His hood, still down, formed a sort of mask; and every time that, in rowing, he spread his arms, from which hung wide black sleeves, they looked like a pair of enormous bat's wings. Moreover, he had not yet uttered a word, a syllable. No other sound was heard in the boat but the working of the oars, and the rippling of the water against the side of the skiff.

The man in black was still struggling against the violent and narrow current that separates the prow of the city from the stern of the Island of Notre-Dame.

'By-the-by, master,' said Gringoire, suddenly, 'just as we reached the Parvis through the raging Truands, did your reverence observe that poor little devil, whose brains your deaf man was dashing out against the balustrade of the gallery of the kings? I am short-sighted, and could not distinguish his features. Who might it be, think you?'

The unknown answered not a word. But he suddenly ceased rowing; his arms dropped as though broken, his head fell upon his breast, and Esmeralda heard him sigh convulsively. She started; she had heard sighs like those before.

The skiff, left to itself, drifted some moments with the stream. But the man in black finally roused himself, seized the oars again, and again set himself to row against the current. He doubled the point of the Island of Notre-Dame, and made for the landing place of the Hay-wharf.

The tumult was increasing around Notre-Dame. They listened. Shouts of victory could very distinctly be heard. Suddenly a hundred flambeaux, that glittered on the helmets of men-at-arms, spread over the church at all heights; on the towers, on the galleries, on the flying buttresses. These torches seemed to be carried in search of something; and soon distant clamors reached distinctly the ears of the fugitives: 'The Egyptian! the sorceress! death to the Egyptian!'

The unhappy creature dropped her head upon her hands, and the unknown began to row furiously towards the bank. Meanwhile, our philosopher reflected. He clasped the goat in his arms, and sidled gently away from the gypsy-girl, who pressed closer and closer to him, as the only protection left her.

It is certain that Gringoire was in a cruel dilemma. He reflected that, as the law then stood, the goat would be hanged too, if she were retaken; that it would be a great pity, poor Djali! that two condemned ones thus clinging to him were too much for him; that, finally, his companion asked nothing better than to take charge of the gypsy. Yet a violent struggle was taking place in his mind; wherein he placed in the balance alternately the gypsy and the goat; and he looked first at one, then at the other, his eyes moist with tears, and saying between his teeth: 'And yet I cannot save you both!'

A shock apprised them that the skiff had reached the shore.

The appalling uproar still rang through the city. The unknown rose, came to the gypsy, and offered to take her arm to assist her to land. She repulsed him, and clung to Gringoire's sleeve, who in turn, absorbed in the goat, almost repulsed her. Then she sprang without help from the boat. She was so disturbed that she knew not what she was doing nor whither she was going. She stood thus for a moment stupefied, watching the water as it flowed. When she recovered herself a little, she found herself alone on the landing-place with the unknown. It appears that Gringoire had taken advantage of the moment of their going ashore to slip away with the goat.

The poor gypsy shuddered on finding herself alone with that man. She strove to speak, to cry out, to call Gringoire; but her tongue refused its office, and not a sound issued from her lips. All at once she felt the hand of the unknown upon hers. It was a cold, strong hand. Her teeth chattered. She turned paler than the moonbeam that shone upon her. The man spoke not a word. He began to move toward the Place de Grève with hasty steps, holding her by the hand. At that moment she had a vague feeling that Fate is an irresistible power. No resistance was left in her; she let him drag along, running while he walked.

The man in black uttered not a syllable. He held her fast, and walked quicker than before. She ceased to resist, and followed him helplessly.

From time to time she mustered a little strength, and said, in a voice broken by the unevenness of the pavement and the breathlessness of their flight: 'Who are you? who are you?' He made no reply.

They arrived thus, keeping still along the quay, at a square of tolerable size. There was then a little moonlight. It was the Grève. In the middle a sort of black cross was visible. It was the gibbet. She recognized all this, and she knew where she was.

The man stopped, turned towards her, and lifted his hood. 'Oh!' faltered she, petrified; 'I knew well that it was he again!'

It was the priest. He looked like the ghost of himself. It was an effect of the moonlight. It seems as if by that light one beholds only the spectres of objects.

'Listen,' said he; and she shuddered at the sound of that fatal voice, which she had not heard for so long. He continued. He spoke with short and panting jerks, which betoken deep internal convulsions. 'Listen. We are here. I have to talk with thee. This is the Grève. This is an extreme point. Fate delivers us up into the hands of each other. I am going to dispose of thy life -- thou, of my soul. Beyond this place and this night nothing is to be foretold. Listen to me, then. I shall tell thee. . . . First, talk to me not of thy Phœbus.' (As he spoke he paced backward and forward like a man incapable of standing still, dragging her after him.) 'Talk not of him. Mark me, if thou utterest his name, I know not what I shall do, but it will be something terrible!'

Then, like a body which recovers its centre of gravity, he became motionless once more; but his words betrayed no less agitation. His voice grew lower and lower.

'Turn not thy head aside so. Hearken to me. 'Tis a serious matter. First, I will tell thee what has happened. There will be no laughing about this, I assure thee. What was I saying? remind me. Ah! it is that there is a decree of the Parliament, delivering thee over to execution again. I have just now taken thee out of their hands. But there they are pursuing thee. Look.'

He stretched out his arm towards the city. The search, in fact, seemed to continue. The uproar drew nearer. The tower of the lieutenant's house, situated opposite to the Grève, was full of noise and lights; and soldiers were running on the opposite quay with torches, shouting: 'The Egyptian! where is the Egyptian? Death! Death!'

'Thou seest plainly,' resumed the priest, 'they are pursuing thee, and that I am not deceiving thee. I love thee. Open not thy lips. Speak not a word, if it be to tell me that thou hatest me. I am determined not to hear that again. I have just now saved thee. First, let me finish. I can save thee absolutely. Everything is prepared. Thou hast only to make it thy wish. As thou wilt, I can do.'

He broke off violently. 'No, that is not what I had to say.'

Then running, and drawing her after him, for he still kept hold of her, he went straight to the gibbet, and pointing to it:

'Choose between us,' said he, coolly.

She tore herself from his grasp, and fell at the foot of the gibbet, grasping that funereal support; then she half turned her beautiful head, and looked at the priest over her shoulder. The priest stood motionless, his finger still raised towards the gibbet, his attitude unchanged, like a statue.

At length the gypsy said to him:

'It is less horrible to me than you are.'

Then he let his arm drop slowly, and cast his eyes upon the ground in deep dejection. 'Could these stones speak,' he murmured, 'yes, they would say, that here stands, indeed, an unhappy man!'

He resumed. The young girl, kneeling before the gibbet, veiled by her long flowing hair, let him speak without interrupting him.

'I love you! Oh, that is still very true! And is nothing, then, perceivable without, of that fire which consumes my heart? Alas! young girl — night and day — yes, night and day! does that deserve no pity? 'Tis a love of the night and the day, I tell you —

'tis torture! Oh, I suffer too much, my poor child, 'tis a thing worthy of compassion, I do assure you. You see that I speak gently to you. I would fain have you cease to abhor me. After all, when a man loves a woman, 'tis not his fault. Oh, my God! What? will you then never pardon me? will you hate me always? and is it all over? 'Tis this that makes me cruel – ay, hateful to myself. You do not even look at me. You are thinking of something else, perchance, while I talk to you as I stand shuddering on the brink of eternity to both of us! Above all, speak not to me of the officer!'

As he uttered these last words, his looks became quite wild. He was silent for a moment; then began again, as if talking to himself, and in a strong voice, 'Cain, what hast thou done with thy brother?'

His eye was haggard, his voice sinking; he repeated several times, mechanically, at considerable intervals, like a bell prolonging its last vibration: 'Because of her, because of her.'

Then his tongue no longer articulated any perceptible sound, though his lips continued to move. All at once he sank down, like something crumbling to pieces, and remained motionless on the ground with his head between his knees.

A slight movement of the young girl, drawing away her foot from under him, brought him to himself. He passed his hand slowly over his hollow cheeks, and gazed for some moments, in vacant astonishment at his fingers, which were wet. 'What?' murmured he, 'have I wept?'

She opened her lips to answer him. He threw himself on his knees before her, to receive with adoration the words, perhaps relenting, which were about to fall from her. She said to him: 'You are an assassin!'

The priest seized her furiously in his arms, and burst into hideous laughter.

'Well, yes, an assassin,' said he, 'and I will have thee. Thou wilt not take me for thy slave; thou shalt have me for thy master. You shall be mine! I have a den, whither I will drag thee. Thou shalt follow me, thou must follow me, or I deliver thee over. Thou must die my fair one, or be mine – the priest's, the apostate's, the assassin's – this very night; dost thou hear? Come, joy! Come! kiss me, silly girl! The grave! or my couch!'

His eyes were sparkling with rage and licentiousness, and his lascivious lips reddened the neck of the young girl. She struggled in his arms. He covered her with furious kisses.

'Do not bite me, monster! she cried. 'Oh, the hateful, poisonous monk! Let me go. I'll pull out thy vile gray hair, and throw it by handfuls in thy face!'

He turned red, then pale, then left hold of her, and gazed upon her gloomily. She thought herself victorious, and continued: 'I tell thee, I belong to my Phœbus, that it is Phœbus I love, that 'tis Phœbus who is handsome! Thou, priest, art old! thou art ugly! Get thee gone!'

He uttered a violent cry, like the wretch to whom a red-hot iron is applied. 'Die, then!' said he, grinding his teeth. She saw his frightful look, and strove to fly. But he seized her again, shook her, threw her upon the ground, and walked rapidly toward the angle of the Tour-Roland, dragging her after him over the pavement by her fair hands.

When he had reached it he turned to her:

'Once for all, wilt thou be mine?'

She answered him with emphasis:

'No!'

Then he called in a loud voice:

'Gudule! Gudule! here's the gypsy-woman! take thy revenge!'

The young girl felt herself seized suddenly by the elbow. She looked; it was a fleshless arm extended through a loop-hole in the wall, and held her with a hand of iron.

'Hold fast!' said the priest; 'it's the gypsy-woman escaped. Do not let her go. I'm going to fetch the sergeants. Thou shalt see her hanged.'

A guttural laugh from the interior of the wall made answer to these deadly words: 'Ha! ha! ha!' The gypsy-girl saw the priest hurry away toward the Pont Notre-Dame. Trampling of horses was heard in that direction.

The young girl had recognized the malicious recluse. Panting with terror, she strove to disengage herself. She writhed. She made several bounds in agony and despair, but the other held her with superhuman strength. The lean, bony fingers that pressed her were clenched and met round her flesh; it seemed as if that hand was riveted to her arm.

'What have I done to you?' said she, almost inarticulately.

'What hast thou done to me, dost thou say? Well, hark thee! I had a child – dost thou see? I had a child; a pretty little girl, my Agnes!' she continued wildly, kissing something in the gloom. 'Well, dost thou see, daughter of Egypt, they took my child from me, they stole my child, they ate my child! That is what thou hast done to me!'

The young girl answered, like the lamb in the fable: 'Alas! perhaps I was not then born!'

'Oh, yes,' rejoined the recluse; 'thou must have been born then. Thou wast one of them; she would have been thy age. For fifteen years have I suffered, fifteen years have I prayed, fifteen years have I been knocking my head against these four walls. I tell thee, they were gypsy-women that stole her from me – dost thou hear that? and who ate her with their teeth. Today it is my turn. I'm going to eat some gypsy-woman's flesh. Oh, how I would bite thee, if the bars did not hinder me; my head is too big. Poor little thing, while she slept! And if they woke her while taking her away, in vain might she cry. I was not there!'

Then she began to laugh or gnash her teeth. The two things resembled each other in that frantic countenance. Day began to dawn. An ashy gleam dimly lighted this scene, and the gibbet grew more and more distinct in the Place. On the other side, towards the bridge of Notre-Dame, the poor victim thought she heard the sound of the horsemen approaching.

'Madame!' she cried, clasping her hands and falling upon her knees, disheveled, distracted, wild with fright, 'madame, have pity! They are coming. I have done nothing to you. Would you have me die that horrible death before your eyes? You are compassionate, I am sure. 'Tis too frightful. Let me fly, let me go. Have mercy! I wish not to die thus!'

'Give me back my little Agnès!' pursued Gudule. 'Thou knowest not where she is? Then, die! I will tell thee! I was once a girl of pleasure; I had a child; they took my child; it was the Egyptian women. Thou seest plainly that thou must die. Stay, let me show thee; here is her shoe, all that is left of her. Dost thou know where its fellow is? If thou dost, tell me; and if it is at the other end of the earth, I'll go thither on my knees to fetch it!'

So saying, with her other arm extended through the aperture, she showed the gypsy the little embroidered shoe. There was already daylight enough to distinguish its shape and color.

The gypsy-girl, starting, said: 'Let me see that shoe. Oh, God! God!'

And at the same time, with the hand she had at liberty, she eagerly opened the little bag with green glass ornaments which she wore about her neck.

'Go on! go on!' grumbled Gudule, 'fumble in thy amulet of the foul fiend —'

She suddenly stopped short, trembled in every limb, and cried in a voice that came from the very depths of her heart: 'My daughter!'

The gypsy had taken out of the bag a little shoe precisely like the other. To this little shoe was attached a slip of parchment, upon which was inscribed this *charm*:

'When thou the like to this shall see,
Thy mother'll stretch her arms to thee.'

Quicker than a flash of lightning the recluse had compared the two shoes, read the inscription on the parchment, and thrust close to the window bars her face, beaming with heavenly joy, crying:

'My daughter! my daughter!'

'My mother!' answered the gypsy-girl.

The wall and the iron bars were between them. 'Oh, the wall!' cried the recluse. 'To see her and not embrace her! Thy hand! thy hand!'

The young girl passed her arm through the opening. The recluse threw herself upon that hand, pressed her lips to it, and there remained, absorbed in that kiss, giving no sign of animation but a sob which heaved her bosom from time to time.

Suddenly she rose, threw back the long gray hair from her face, and without saying a word, strove with both hands, and with the fury of a lioness, to shake the bars of her window hole. The bars were firm. She then went and fetched from one corner of her cell a large paving-stone, which served her for a pillow, and hurled it against them with such violence that one of the bars broke, casting numberless sparks. A second stroke drove out the old iron cross that barricaded the window. Then, with both hands, she managed to loosen and remove the rusty stumps of the bars.

The passage clear – and it was all done in less than a minute – she seized her daughter by the middle of her body and drew her into the cell. 'Come,' murmured she, 'let me drag thee out of the abyss!'

'My daughter! my daughter!' she said; 'I have my daughter! Here she is! The good God has given her back to me!'

'Oh, my mother!' said the young girl, gathering strength at last to speak in her emotion; 'the gypsy-woman told me so. There was a good gypsy among our people who died last year, and she had always taken care of me like a foster-mother. It was she that had put this little bag on my neck. She used always to say to me: "Little one, guard this trinket well; 'tis a treasure; it will enable thee to find thy mother again. Thou wearest thy mother about thy neck." She foretold it – the gypsy-woman.'

Again the Sachette clasped her daughter in her arms.

At that moment the cell resounded with a clattering of arms and galloping of horses, which seemed to be advancing from the bridge of Notre-Dame, and approaching nearer and nearer along the quay. The gypsy threw herself in agony into the arms of the Sachette: 'Save me! save me! my mother! they are coming!'

The recluse turned pale again.

'Oh, heaven! what dost thou say? I had forgotten. They are pursuing thee. What hast thou done, then?'

'I know not,' replied the unfortunate child, 'but I am condemned to die.'

'To die!' exclaimed Gudule, reeling as if struck by a thunderbolt. 'To die!' she repeated slowly, gazing at her daughter with a fixed stare.

'Yes, my mother,' repeated the young girl, with wild despair, 'they want to kill me. They are coming to hang me. That gallows is for me. Save me! save me! They are coming. Save me!'

Here the cavalcade appeared to halt, and a distant voice was heard saying:

'This way, Messire Tristan. The priest says we shall find her at the Rat-hole.' The tramp of the horses began again.

The recluse started up with a shriek of despair:

'Fly, fly, my child! It all comes back to me. Thou art right. 'Tis thy death! horror! malediction! fly!'

She put her head to the loop-hole, and drew it back again hastily.

'Stay,' said she, in an accent low, brief and doleful, pressing convulsively the hand of the gypsy, who was more dead than alive. 'Stay where you are. Do not breathe. There are soldiers everywhere. Thou canst not get away. It is too light.'

Her eyes were dry and burning. For a moment she said nothing, only paced the cell hurriedly, stopping now and then to pluck out handfuls of gray hair, which she afterwards tore with her teeth.

All at once she said: 'They are coming. I will speak to them. Hide thyself in that corner. They will not see thee. I will tell them thou hast escaped; that I let thee go, i' faith.'

She set down her daughter (for she was still carrying her) in one corner of the cell which was not visible from without. She made her crouch down; arranged her carefully, so that neither foot nor hand should project from the shadow; unbound her black hair, and spread it over her white robe, to conceal it; and placed before her the water-jug and paving-stone – the only articles of furniture she had – imagining that this jug and stone would hide her.

At that moment, the voice of the priest – that infernal voice – passed very near the cell, crying:

'This way, Captain Phœbus de Chateaupers.'

At that name, at that voice, Esmeralda, crouching in her corner, made a movement.

'Stir not,' said Gudule.

Scarcely had she said this before a tumultuous crowd of men, swords and horses, stopped around the cell. The mother rose quickly, and went and posted herself at the loop-hole, to cover the aperture. She beheld a large troop of armed men, horse and foot, drawn up on the Grève. The commander dismounted and came toward her.

'Old woman,' said this man, who had an atrocious face, 'we are in search of a witch, to hang her. We were told that thou hadst her.'

The poor mother, assuming as indifferent a look as she could, replied:

'I don't quite know what you mean.'

The other resumed: 'Tête-Dieu! Then what sort of a tale was that crazy archdeacon telling us? Where is he?'

'Monseigneur,' said a soldier, 'he has disappeared.'

'Come, now, old mad woman,' resumed the commander, 'tell me no lies. A sorceress was given you to keep. What have you done with her?'

The recluse, not wishing to deny all, for fear of awakening suspicion, replied, in a sincere and surly tone:

'If you mean a tall young girl that was given me to hold just now, I can tell you that she bit me, and I let her go. There! Leave me in peace.'

The commander made a grimace of disappointment.

'Let me have no lying, old spectre,' he said. 'And which way did she take?'

Gudule answered carelessly: 'By the Rue du Mouton, I believe.'

Tristan turned his head, and motioned to his men to prepare to march. The recluse breathed again.

'Monseigneur,' said an archer all at once, 'just ask the old elf how it is that her window-bars are broken out so?'

This question brought anguish again to the heart of the miserable mother. Still she did not lose all presence of mind. 'They were always so,' stammered she.

'Pshaw!' returned the archer; 'they formed but yesterday a fine black cross that made a man feel devout.'

Tristan cast an oblique glance at the recluse.

'I think the old crone is confused,' said he.

The unfortunate woman felt that all depended on her self-possession; and so, with death in her soul, she began to jeer.

'Bah!' said she, 'the man is drunk. 'Tis more than a year since the back of a cart laden with stones backed against my window and broke the grating. And how I cursed the driver!'

'If a cart had done that,' resumed the first soldier, 'the stumps of the bars would be driven inward, whereas they have been forced outward.'

'Ha! ha!' said Tristan to the soldier, 'thou hast the nose of an inquisitor at the Châtelet. Answer what he says, old woman.'

'Good heavens!' exclaimed she, driven to bay, and with tears in her voice in spite of herself, 'I swear to you, monseigneur, that it was a cart which broke those bars.'

Tristan shook his head. She turned pale.

'How long is it, say you, since this cart affair?' he asked.

'A month, perhaps a fortnight, monseigneur. I cannot recollect exactly.'

'She said at first above a year,' observed the soldier.

'Monseigneur,' cried she, still standing close to the opening, and trembling lest suspicion should prompt them to thrust in their heads and look into the cell – 'monseigneur, I swear to you that 'twas a cart which broke this grating; I swear it to you by all the angels in paradise. If it was not done by a cart, I wish I may go to everlasting perdition, and I deny my God!'

'Thou art very hot in that oath of thine,' said Tristan with his inquisitorial glance.

The poor woman felt her assurance forsaking her more and more. She was already making blunders, and she perceived with terror that she was not saying what she should have said.

Another soldier now came up, crying:

'Monseigneur, the old elf lies. The sorceress has not gotten away by the Rue du Mouton. The chain of that street has been stretched across all night, and the chain-keeper has seen nobody go by.'

The poor child had been all this time in her corner, without breathing or stirring; with the image of death staring her in the face. No particular of the scene between Gudule and Tristan had escaped her; she had shared all the agonies endured by her mother. She had heard, as it were, each successive cracking of the thread which had held her suspended over the abyss. At this moment she heard a voice saying to the provost:

'Cor-bœuf! monsieur the provost, 'tis no business of mine, who am a guardsman, to hang sorceresses. The rabble of the populace is put down. I leave you to do your own work by yourself. You will permit me to rejoin my company, since it is without a captain.'

The voice was that of Phœbus de Chateaupers. What took place within her was indescribable. He was there, her friend, her protector, her support, her shelter, her Phœbus! She started up; and before her mother could prevent her, she had sprung to the window, crying:

'Phœbus! hither! my Phœbus!'

Phœbus was no longer there. He had just galloped round the corner of the Rue de la Coutellerie. But Tristan was not yet gone.

The recluse rushed upon her daughter with the roar of a wild beast; she dragged her violently back, her nails entering the flesh of the poor girl's neck. A tigress mother does not stand on trifles. But it was too late. Tristan had seen.

'Ha, ha,' he cried, with a grin which showed all his teeth, and made his face resemble that of a wolf, 'two mice in the trap.'

'I suspected as much,' said the soldier.

Tristan slapped him on the shoulder:

'Thou art a good cat! Come,' he added, 'where is Henriet Cousin?'

A man who had neither the garb nor the mien of a soldier, stepped forth from the ranks. He wore a dress half gray, half brown, had lank hair, leathern sleeves and a coil of rope in his huge fist.

'Friend,' said Tristan l'Hermite, 'I presume that yonder is the sorceress whom we are seeking. Thou wilt hang me this one. Hast thou thy ladder?'

'There is one under the shed of the Maison-aux-Piliers,' replied the man. 'Is it on this *justice* that the thing is to be done?' continued he, pointing to the stone gibbet.

'Yes.'

'So, ho!' said the man, with a loud laugh, more brutal still than that of the provost, 'we shall not have far to go!'

Meanwhile, since Tristan had seen her daughter, and all hope was lost, the recluse had not uttered a word. She had flung the poor gypsy, half dead, into the corner of the cell, and had posted herself again at the loop-hole, both hands resting upon the edge of the stone sill, like two claws. In this attitude her eyes, which had again become wild and fierce, were seen to wander fearlessly over the surrounding soldiers. When Henriet Cousin approached her place, her look was so ferocious that he started back.

'Monseigneur,' said he, turning back to the provost, 'which are we to take?'

'The young one.'

'So much the better, for the old one seemeth difficult.'

Henriet Cousin again approached the window-hole. The mother's eye made his own droop. He said with some timidity:

'Madame – '

She interrupted him in a very low but furious voice: 'What wouldst thou?'

'Not you,' said he, 'but the other.'

'What other?'

'The young one.'

She began to shake her head, crying:

'There is no one! no one! no one!'

'I tell you there is,' rejoined the hangman. 'We've all seen that there are two of you.'

'You look, then,' said the recluse, with her strange sneer.

Thrust your head through the window.'

The hangman eyed the mother's nails, and durst not venture.
'Monseigneur,' he asked, 'how must I get in?'

'Through the door.'

'There is none.'

'Through the window, then.'

'It's not wide enough.'

'Widen it then,' said Tristan, angrily. 'Hast thou no picks?'

Henriet Cousin went to fetch the box of tools from under
the shed of the Pillar House. He also brought from the same
place the double ladder, which he immediately set up against
the gibbet. Five or six of the provost's men provided themselves
with picks and crowbars, and Tristan went with them to the
window of the cell.

'Old woman,' said the provost, in a tone of severity, 'give up
the girl quietly.'

She looked at him as one who does not understand.

'God's head!' added Tristan; 'what good can it do thee to
hinder that witch from being hanged as it pleases the king?'

The wretched woman burst into her wild laugh.

'What good can it do me? She is my daughter!'

The tone in which this word was uttered produced a shudder
even in Henriet Cousin.

To make an opening sufficiently large, it was only necessary
to remove one course of stone underneath the window. When
the mother heard the picks and the levers undermining her
fortress, she uttered a dreadful cry. Then she began to circle
with frightful quickness round and round her cell – a habit of
a wild beast, which her long residence in the cage had given her.
She said nothing more, but her eyes were flaming. The soldiers
felt their blood chilled to the very heart.

All at once she took up her paving-stone, laughed and threw
it with both hands at the workmen. The stone, ill-aimed (for her
hands were trembling), touched no one, but fell harmless at the
feet of Tristan's horse. She gnashed her teeth.

The crowbars now raised the heavy course of stone. It was the
mother's last bulwark. She threw herself upon it, she would fain
have held it in its place, she scratched the stones with her nails,
but the heavy mass, put in motion by six men, escaped her
grasp, and fell gently to the ground along the iron levers.

The mother, seeing the breach effected, threw herself on the
floor across the opening, barricading it with her body, writhing
her arms, beating her head against the flag-stone and crying in
a voice, hoarse and nearly inarticulate from exhaustion: 'Help,
help! fire, fire!'

The executioner and the sergeants entered the cell. The mother could make no resistance; she only dragged up to her daughter and clasped her madly. When the gypsy-girl saw the soldiers approaching, the horror of death revived.

'My mother!' cried she, in a tone of indescribable distress; 'oh, my mother! they are coming; defend me!'

'Yes, my love, I am defending thee!' answered the mother, in a faint voice; and clasping her close to her arms, she covered her with kisses.

Henriet Cousin took the gypsy-girl by the body, just below her beautiful shoulders. When she felt his hands touching her, she cried out and fainted. The executioner, from whose eye big tears were falling upon her drop by drop, offered to carry her away in his arms. He strove to unclasp the embrace of the mother, who had, as it were, knotted her hands about her daughter's waist; but the grasp which thus bound her to her child was so powerful that he found it impossible to part them. Henriet Cousin therefore dragged the young girl out of the cell, and her mother after her. The eyes of the mother were also closed.

The sun was rising at that moment; and already there was a considerable collection of people in the square, looking from a distance to see what they were thus dragging over the pavement toward the gibbet.

There was nobody at the windows. Only far away, on the top of that one of the towers of Notre-Dame which looks upon the Grève, two men could be seen who stood darkly out against the clear morning sky, and who seemed to be looking on.

Henriet Cousin paused with the object he was dragging, at the foot of the fatal ladder; and, with troubled breath (so strongly was he moved to pity), he passed the rope around the young lovely neck. The unfortunate girl felt the horrible contact of the hempen cord. She raised her eyelids, and beheld the skeleton arm of the stone gibbet extended over her head. Then she shook off her torpor, and cried, in a loud and agonizing voice: 'No! no! I will not!' The mother, whose head was buried by her daughter's garments, said not a word; but her entire body was convulsed, and she was heard redoubling her kisses upon the form of her child. The executioner seized that moment to unclasp, by a strong and sudden effort, the arms with which she held fast the prisoner, and, whether from exhaustion or despair, they yielded. He then took the young girl upon his shoulder, from whence her charming figure fell gracefully bending over his large head, and set his foot upon the ladder in order to ascend.

At this instant, the mother, who had sunk upon the ground, opened wide her eyes. Without uttering a cry, she started up with a terrific expression upon her face; then, like a beast rushing upon its prey, she threw herself upon the executioner's hand, and set her teeth in it. It was like a flash of lightning. The executioner howled with pain. They ran to his relief, and with difficulty liberated his bleeding hand from the teeth of the mother. She kept a profound silence. They pushed her away with brutal violence, and it was remarked that her head fell back heavily upon the ground. They raised her; she fell back again. She was dead.

The hangman, who had not loosed his hold of the young girl, kept on up the ladder.

2

When Quasimodo saw that the cell was empty; that the gypsy-girl was no longer there; that, while he had been defending her, she had been abducted, he took his head between his hands and stamped with rage and astonishment. Then he began to run over all the church, seeking his Bohemian, howling strange cries at every corner, strewing his red hair on the pavement. It was just at the moment when the king's archers were making their victorious entry into Notre-Dame, likewise in search of the gypsy-girl. Quasimodo assisted them, having no suspicion, poor deaf creature, of their fatal intentions; he thought that the enemies of the Egyptians were the Truands. He himself took Tristan l'Hermite to every possible hiding-place; opened for him all the secret doors, the double backs to the altars, the inner sacristies. Had the unfortunate girl still been there, he himself would have delivered her up to them,

When the irksomeness of seeking in vain had discouraged Tristan, who was not easily discouraged, Quasimodo continued the search alone. Twenty times, a hundred times over, did he make the circuit of the church, from one end to the other, from top to bottom – ascending, descending, running, calling, shouting, peeping, rummaging, ferreting, putting his head into every hole, thrusting a torch under every arch, desperate, mad, haggard and moaning like a beast that has lost its mate.

At length, when he was sure, perfectly sure, that she was gone, that all was over, that she had been stolen from him, he slowly went up the steps of the tower, the steps that he had mounted so nimbly and triumphantly on the day he saved her. The church was again deserted and silent as before. The archers had quitted it to track the sorceress in the city. Quasimodo, left alone in that vast Notre-Dame, but a moment before besieged and full of tumult, betook himself once more to the cell where the gypsy had slept for so many weeks under his protection.

As he approached it, he could not help fancying that he might, perhaps, find her there. When, at the turn of the gallery which opens on the roof of the side aisle, he could see the narrow little lodging, with its small window and tiny door, sheltered under one of the great buttresses, like a bird's nest under a bough, the poor fellow's heart failed him, and he leaned against a pillar to keep from falling.

At last he summoned up courage, approached on tip-toe, looked, entered. Empty! the cell was still empty! The unhappy man paced slowly round it, lifted up her couch, and looked underneath it, as if she could have been hidden between the mattress and the stones; he then shook his head and stood stupefied. All at once he furiously trampled upon his torch, and without word or sigh, he rushed at full speed head-foremost against the wall, and fell senseless upon the floor.

When he recovered his senses he threw himself on the bed, rolled upon it and frantically kissed the place, still warm, where the damsel had lain; he remained thus for some minutes, as motionless as if life had fled; he then rose, bathed in perspiration, panting, beside himself, and fell to beating his head against the wall with the frightful regularity of a pendulum, and the resolution of a man determined to dash out his brains. At length he sank exhausted a second time. Presently he crawled on his knees out of the cell, and crouched down opposite the door in an attitude of astonishment.

He remained thus for more than an hour, his eye fixed upon the deserted cell, more gloomy and thoughtful than a mother seated between an empty cradle and a full coffin. He uttered not a word; only at long intervals a sob shook violently his whole body; but it was a sobbing without tears, like summer lightning, which makes no noise.

It appears to have been then that, seeking amid his desolate thoughts to discover who could have been the unexpected abductor of the gypsy-girl, he bethought himself of the archdeacon. He recollected that Dom Claude alone possessed a key to the staircase leading to the cell; he remembered his nocturnal attempts upon La Esmeralda, the first of which he, Quasimodo, had assisted, the second of which he had prevented. He called to mind a thousand details, and soon no longer doubted that the archdeacon had taken the gypsy-girl from him. Yet such was his reverence for the priest, gratitude, devotion and love for that man were so deeply rooted in his heart, that they resisted, even at this dire moment, the fangs of jealousy and despair.

He reflected that the archdeacon had done this thing, and that sanguinary, deadly resentment which he would have felt against any other individual, was turned in the poor deaf man's breast, the moment when Claude Frollo was in question, into simply an increase of sorrow.

At the moment that his thoughts were thus fixed on the priest, while the buttresses were beginning to whiten in the dawn, he descried, on the upper gallery of Notre-Dame, at the angle formed by the external balustrade which runs round the apsis, a figure walking. It was the archdeacon. Claude walked with a slow, grave step. He did not look before him as he went; he was going toward the northern tower, but his face was turned to the right bank of the Seine; and he carried his head erect, as if striving to obtain a view of something over the roofs. In this manner the priest passed above Quasimodo without seeing him.

Quasimodo went up the steps of the tower, to ascend it and to ascertain why the priest went up. The poor ringer knew not what he was going to do (he, Quasimodo), what he was going to say, what he wanted. He was full of rage and full of dread. The archdeacon and the Egyptian came into conflict in his heart.

When he reached the top of the tower, before he issued from the darkness of the stairs upon the open platform, he cautiously observed the whereabouts of the priest. The priest had his back toward him. An open-work balustrade surrounds the platform of the spire. The priest, whose eyes were bent upon the town, was leaning his breast upon the one of the four sides of the balustrade which looks upon the bridge of Notre-Dame.

Quasimodo stole with the stealthy tread of a wolf behind him to see at what he was thus gazing.

The priest's attention was so completely absorbed elsewhere that he heard not the step of the hunchback near him.

Quasimodo burned to ask him what he had done with the gypsy-girl, but the archdeacon seemed at that moment to be out of the world. He was visibly in one of those critical moments of life when one would not feel the earth crumble.

With his eyes steadily fixed on a certain spot, he remained motionless and silent; and in that silence and immobility there was something so formidable that the untamed bell-ringer shuddered at it, and dared not intrude upon it. Only (and this was one way of interrogating the archdeacon) he followed the direction of his eye; and, thus guided, that of the unhappy hunchback fell upon the Place de Grève.

He thus discovered what the priest was looking at. The ladder was set up against the permanent gibbet. There were a few people in the Place, and a number of soldiers. A man was dragging along the ground something white, to which something black was clinging. This man stopped at the foot of the gibbet. Here something took place which Quasimodo could not clearly see, a group of soldiers prevented his seeing everything.

The man began to mount the ladder. Quasimodo now saw him distinctly again. He was carrying a woman on his shoulder – a young girl clad in white. That young girl had a noose about her neck. Quasimodo recognized her.

It was she!

The man reached the top of the ladder. There he arranged the noose. Here the priest, in order to see better, knelt upon the balustrade.

Suddenly the man pushed away the ladder with his heel, and Quasimodo, who had not breathed for some moments, beheld the unfortunate child dangling at the end of the rope, about two fathoms above the ground, with the man squatted upon her shoulders. The rope made several gyrations on itself, and Quasimodo beheld horrible convulsions run along the gypsy's body.

At the most awful moment, a demoniacal laugh, a laugh such as can come only from one who is no longer human, burst from the livid visage of the priest. Quasimodo did not hear that laugh, but he saw it.

The ringer retreated a few steps behind the archdeacon, and then, suddenly rushing furiously upon him with his huge hands, he pushed him by the back into the abyss over which Dom Claude was leaning.

The priest shrieked, 'Damnation!' and fell.

The spout, above which he stood, arrested his fall. He clung to it with desperate grip; but, at the moment when he opened his mouth to give a second cry, he beheld the formidable and avenging face of Quasimodo thrust over the edge of the balustrade above his head. Then he was silent.

The abyss was beneath him, a fall of full two hundred feet – and the pavement.

In this dreadful situation the archdeacon said not a word, breathed not a groan. Only he writhed upon the gutter, making incredible efforts to re-ascend; but his hands had no hold on the granite, his feet slid along the blackened wall without catching hold.

Quasimodo had but to stretch out his hand to draw him from the gulf, but he did not so much as look at him. He was looking at the Grève, he was looking at the gibbet, he was looking at the gypsy.

The deaf man was leaning with his elbows on the balustrade, at the very spot where the archdeacon had been a moment before, and there, never turning his eye from the only object which existed for him at that moment, he was mute and motionless, like one struck by lightning, and a long stream of tears flowed in silence from that eye which until then shed but one.

Meanwhile the archdeacon was panting; his bald brow was dripping with perspiration; his nails were bleeding against the stones; the skin was rubbed from his knees against the wall.

He heard his cassock, which was caught on the spout, crack and rip with each jerk that he gave it. To complete his misfortune, this spout ended in a leaden pipe, which he could feel slowly bending under the weight of his body. The wretched man said to himself, that when his hands should be worn out with fatigue, when his cassock should tear asunder, when the leaden pipe should yield, he must of necessity fall, and horror thrilled his very vitals. Now and then he glanced wildly at a sort of narrow ledge formed, some ten feet lower, by projections in the sculpture; and he implored heaven from the bottom of his agonized soul, that he might be permitted to spend the remainder of his life upon that narrow space of two feet square, though it were to last a hundred years.

There was something frightful in the silence of these two men. While the archdeacon struggled with death in this horrible manner, but a few feet from him, Quasimodo looked at the Grève and wept.

The archdeacon, finding that all his exertions served but to shake the only frail support left to him, at length remained quite still. There he hung, clasping the gutter, scarcely breathing, no longer stirring, without any other motion than that mechanical convulsion of the stomach, which one experiences in a dream when one fancies himself falling. His fixed eyes were wide open with a stare of pain and astonishment. Little by little, however, he lost ground; his fingers slipped along the spout; he felt more and more the weakness of his arms and the weight of his body; the leaden pipe which supported him bent more and more every moment towards the abyss. He saw beneath him, frightful sight, the sharp roof of the church of Saint-Jean-de-Rond, as small as a card bent double.

Quasimodo wept.

At length the archdeacon, foaming with rage and horror, became sensible that all was in vain. Nevertheless, he gathered what strength remained to him for one last effort. He straightened himself on the gutter, set both knees against the wall, clung with his hands to a cleft in the stone-work and succeeded in climbing up, perhaps, one foot; but this struggle caused the leaden beak which supported him to give way suddenly. The same effort rent his cassock asunder. Then, finding everything under him giving way, having only his stiffened and crippled hands to hold by, the unhappy wretch closed his eyes and let go of the spout. He fell.

Quasimodo watched him falling.

A fall from such a height is seldom perpendicular. The archdeacon, launched into space, fell at first with his head downward and his arms extended, then he turned over several times. The wind blew him upon the roof of a house, where the miserable man broke some of his bones. Nevertheless, he was not dead when he reached it. The ringer could perceive him still make an effort to cling to the gable with his hands, but the slope was too steep, and he had no strength left. He glided rapidly down the roof like a loosened tile, then rebounded on the pavement; there he stirred no more.

Quasimodo then lifted his eye to the gypsy, whose body, suspended from the gibbet, he beheld afar, quivering under its white robe, in the last agonies of death; then he looked at the archdeacon, stretched a shapeless mass at the foot of the tower, and he said, with a sob that heaved his deep breast: 'Oh! all that I have ever loved!'

About a year and a half or two years after the events with which this history concludes, when search was made in the vault of Montfaucon for the body of Olivier le Daim, who had been hanged two days before, and to whom Charles VIII granted the favor of being buried in Saint Laurent in better company, there were found among all those hideous carcasses, two skeletons, one of which held the other in a singular embrace. One of these skeletons, which was that of a woman, had still about it some tattered fragments of a garment, that had once been white; and about the neck was a string of adrezarach beads, with a little silken bag, ornamented with green glass, which was open and empty. These objects were of so little value that the executioner had probably not cared to take them. The other, which held this one in a close embrace, was the skeleton of a man. It was noticed that the spine was crooked, the head depressed between the shoulders, and that one leg was shorter than the other. Moreover, there was no rupture of the vertebrae at the nape of the neck, whence it was evident that he had not been hanged. Hence the man to whom it belonged must have come thither and have died there. When they strove to detach this skeleton from the one it was embracing it crumbled to dust.